I AM Lucy

LUCY SMOLČIĆ

Copyright © 2019 Lucy Smolčić

All rights reserved.

ISBN: 9781698264424

DEDICATION

To Kris and Mia.
To Marija and James.
To myself.

To all men, women and children who haven't had a voice.

Hvala Ma i Ta.
Hvala svima u Hrvatsku što ste me primili kao svoje.

This is a Public Service Book.
This is My True Story.

Book One - I am Lucy, Far Away From Here

I wrote my first version of this book live on FaceBook to begin to try to understand how I ever got to a point in life where I allowed myself and my children to live a life of extreme, traumatic abuse. I wrote to understand myself and search for answers so that I never live in fear again and to break the cycle. To break the belief that I felt and truly believed I deserved to be mistreated, used and abused. To understand how to live a life of self-respect and self-worth, I needed to be honest with myself and with others. This book has been revised from the original FaceBook version but for the most part is the same.

This first book, I am Lucy, is my journey in seeking true freedom and to escape not only the abusive patterns, but to escape my own thoughts and beliefs which allowed me to enter and stay in a life that no one on this Earth should ever live. In hopes to not only help others but to help myself, I am self-publishing this book and understand it's not perfect. It hasn't been seen by a real Editor and in no way will be perfect. This is the way it's intended to be read. Imperfect, just as I am and am now proud to be. Breaking the cycle of abuse means breaking the belief there is a certain preset way to do things. Publishing this book on my own is one of my challenges as I am not used to allowing imperfection in my world.

Thank you to all who were a part of my FaceBook journey and all who were behind the scenes as well. I have a long road ahead of me but I am becoming a person I am proud of.

I'm not a victim. I'm not a warrior.
I'm who I choose and allow myself to be.
I am Lucy.

Book Two - Currently being written

In Book Two, currently untitled, I am writing of the details specifically between 2014 to present day. This book should be complete either by Christmas 2019 or early in the New Year 2020. This book will include details of the nine charges against Alen, the upcoming charges to be laid, my journey following escape, life through the legal system as well as the trial set for three days in December 2019. It will describe many battles we had to endure even after leaving abuse. It will shed light on the reality that there was not a feeling of true escape and the legal system supported the continued abuse towards us. It will describe many things while showing how to continue on the path to what is everyone's right, to be free and to be respected. To fight for what's right.

Book Three

Book Three, I intend to write of a beautiful life I live full of freedom, love, peace and respect. My life while I wrote Book One or as I write Book Two is not the way to live life. It's only the process I had to endure and fight through in order to, in the end, live my life and the life I truly deserve. A life that belongs to me.

This is a Public Service true story.

TABLE OF CONTENTS

1 PART ONE	3
1992 Ivankovo, Croatia	3
Far Away From Here	3
2 PART TWO	6
1992 Ivankovo, Croatia	6
The Simplicity of A Smile	6
3 PART THREE	12
1992 Ivankovo, Croatia	12
Life Experiences and Lessons Learned	12
4 PART FOUR	19
1992 Ivankovo, Croatia	19
Life Continues Even in War	19
5 PART FIVE	23
1992 Ivankovo, Croatia	23
Meeting Milan	23
6 PART SIX	27
1992 Ivankovo, Croatia	27
Looking Back	27
7 PART SEVEN	32
1992 Ivankovo, Croatia	32
I Never Wanted to Leave	32
8 PART EIGHT	39
1992 Calgary, Canada	39
A Stranger in My Hometown	39
9 PART NINE	45
Christmas Eve 1997 To May 15, 1999	45
Calgary, Canada	45
Had I Known, I Would Have Run Away	45
10 PART TEN	53

1999 Calgary, Canada 53

The Mirror Saw My Pain 53

11 PART ELEVEN 59

1999 Calgary, Canada 59

The Process of Acceptance and Owning My Decisions 59

12 PART TWELVE 66

1999-2000 Calgary, Canada 66

I Was Happy Enough 66

13 PART THIRTEEN 74

2005 Conrich, Canada 74

Finally, I Fell Apart 74

14 PART FOURTEEN 87

2007 87

The Life I Was Shown to Live 87

15 PART FIFTEEN 102

2009 102

A Demon Towering Over Me 102

16 PART SIXTEEN 106

2019 106

Ten Years Gone By. Broken Road to Freedom. 106

17 PART SEVENTEEN 112

My kids and I fled our lives in Domestic Violence, Abuse and Control for the Very Last Time on December 24, 2018. Christmas Eve. 112

18 PART EIGHTEEN 121

The Mountains Protected Us 121

19 PART NINETEEN 125

Courage to Change the Things I Can 125

20 PART TWENTY 130

I Couldn't Tell Them the Truth 130

21 PART TWENTY ONE 136

The Silent One Goes Crazy. 136

The Crazy One Goes Silent. 136

22 PART TWENTY TWO 142

Once Upon A Time: The Truth and Nothing but the Truth 142

23 PART TWENTY THREE...146

Writing This Book...146

24 PART TWENTY FOUR 151

Searching for the Root Cause of Wrong..151

25 PART TWENTY FIVE 158

I Promise to Speak the Truth and Nothing But, Forever and Always, No Matter What 158

26 PART TWENTY SIX...162

RCMP did everything they could to keep us safe and I trust them. The abuse continued even still and within the law, our very own legal system. This is termed Legal Harassment and is quite simply, abuse supported and enforced within the law, Family Law. 162

PART TWENTY SEVEN 173

A Part of Me Fell Apart But I am Not Broken 173

Freedom..173

…Everything that led to my coming here… 176

MY SON SAVED MY LIFE..177

MY DAUGHTER SAVED MY LIFE...179

WRITTEN BY MY DAUGHTER MIA AFTER FLEEING AN EXTREMELY ABUSIVE HOME AND FREE TO BEGIN TO SPEAK HER TRUTH AT 16 YEARS OF AGE. 181

I AM Lucy Smolcic

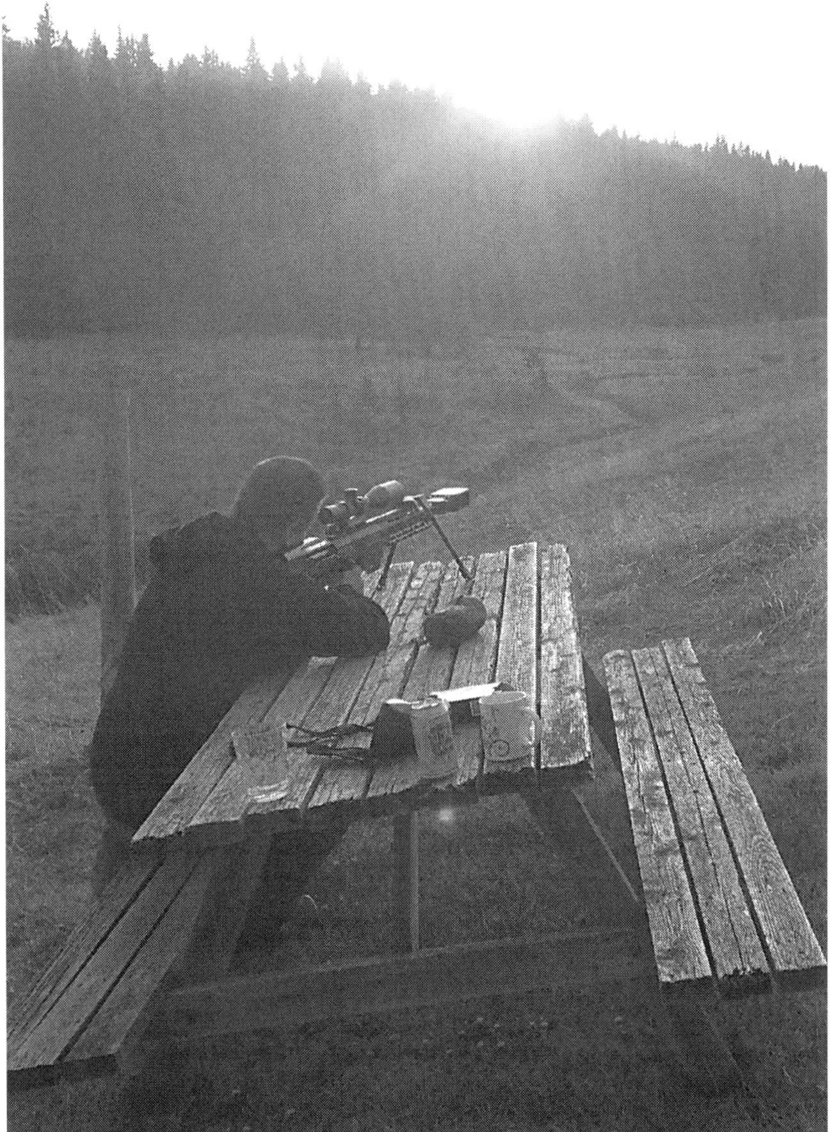

ALL PROCEEDS FROM THIS BOOK GO TO SUPPORT MY CHILDREN.

Written By © Lucy Smolcic 2019

Photo Credits to:
Book Cover and various photos throughout the book
© Mia Mango

Ivankovo the Village
Friends and Family

Book Cover Design Credit to:
© Marija Smolcic

Let them have their stories.
Mine's true.

I am Lucy

······. If only I were able to be ······.

FAR AWAY FROM HERE

Photo By © Mia Mango 2019

I AM Lucy

Ivankovo, Croatia village center.

*Me in 1992 in my neighbour's store.
Ivankovo, Croatia*

1 PART ONE
1992 Ivankovo, Croatia
Far Away From Here

....Everything that led to my coming here, to this tiny village on this night, was not making much sense. I always knew I needed to go to an extreme in life to really understand the emotions that are part of my being. I believed no one really understood me or my intense feelings. Especially back home in Canada. I didn't fit in to the regular teenage life and I definitely didn't want to go through life being numb to what I believed to be, the real world. I had turned 18 just months before and felt as though I was going on 50.

Ivankovo, Croatia. They explained it to be a village, not a town and definitely not a city. The houses made of cement or a stone of some sort, lined the narrow roads fitting snug against one another with only a few feet between them. Large iron fences and gates separated their yards from the sidewalk and metal shutters covered each window. Old. They were all so old. Nothing like I could have ever seen had I stayed in Canada. The scent in the air was also something I could never really explain to anyone. The smell of the country was different than any I had ever noticed before. It was a nice scent, not uncomfortable at all, but definitely unusual and difficult to pin down. The scent, the roads, the houses. Everything was sort of surreal.

My Aunt Kate and her husband Mark would provide me with a temporary home away from home over the next few months. She was my Dad's oldest sister and welcomed me into her home quite simply, I believe, because I gave her no choice. I just showed up and had nowhere else to stay, and well, she offered, and I quickly accepted the invitation.

After a full day of meeting Aunts and cousins and neighbours, and after a full day of answering a hundred questions of "*What are you doing here?*", "*Why would you come now?*" and "*I can't believe a Canadian is in Ivankovo*", I finally found comfort in my new bed. It was well past midnight, I thought, and the skies were black with little stars.

My room was the closest facing the road and farthest from the kitchen. No heat throughout the house, only a wooden stove could provide any comfort from the cold, and of course, it was in the kitchen. I bundled myself up tight in a feather quilt my Aunt must have made by hand and reached for my walkman. For years, I had been falling asleep to the sound of music. Back home, I had a radio by my bed and there was always music to send me into a dreamy sleep. Now, my walkman would have to replace my radio.

With the headset lightly over my head and both earphones tight against my ears, I listened to a tape of slow, soft tunes. I felt all the pressure and nerves from the day easing and slowly, I relaxed and began falling into my beautiful sleepy state. Life was changing and I knew that every day from that moment on, would be something new and exciting.

Just as I was about to sleep, I jumped up and into a sitting position in my bed and felt my heart pounding right through my clothes. It was loud and fast and raced. I looked down to my chest and I'm positive I could actually see the pulse moving my shirt while my wrists ached from the racing of my heartbeat. My bed was shaking, literally, moving! The soft music suddenly became piercing and annoying and interfered with my perception and ability to get a hold of myself. I grabbed my headset and flung it across the room. I tried to stop breathing so I could hear. I couldn't hear! My panic seemed to overcome me and I couldn't see, couldn't hear, couldn't understand what was happening.

As my bed began to shake again I finally heard a deep grumbling sound. With every grumble, my bed shook again. I jumped from my bed and ran through the bedroom door into my Aunt's room. She looked startled to find me there in a panic. I was startled to find her there calmly lying down!

I cleared my throat and felt a bit embarrassed for my reaction and asked as calmly as I possibly could, "What is that?"

"Oh, don't worry, that's far away from here." She replied with a small giggle.

"Far away from here," I whispered. "What, is far away from here?" I asked, once again, trying to remain calm.

"The bombs. They must be landing someplace else. It's nothing to worry about, go back to bed." With that, she smiled and closed her eyes as she turned to face the opposite wall. And with that, I stood for a few more seconds, then realized she really was going back to sleep, so I turned and left her room.

Far away from here.....that replayed in my mind over and again for at least hours afterward, as I sat in my bed, covered with my feather filled quilt, walkman now completely shut off and on the table....skies grumbling, bed trembling....trying to understand....nothing to worry about, far away from here.

Me in Vinkovci, Croatia 1996

Me in Vinkovci, Croatia

2 PART TWO
1992 IVANKOVO, CROATIA
THE SIMPLICITY OF A SMILE

I could sense slits of sunlight shining through the metal shutter covering my window falling warmly on my cheeks. My eyes were still closed as I rubbed them awake. I stretched and turned to bring myself up and sitting on my bed. As I slowly began to open my sleepy eyes, I smelled the scent I would eventually take for granted. Ivankovo, I was still there and I was alright. The night before I knew I must have fallen asleep while I could sense slits of sunlight shining through the metal shutter covering my window falling warmly on my cheeks.

The night before I knew I must have fallen asleep while the earth still grumbled and shook my bed. I was thankful that I did. This new day had begun with a beautiful calm sense and I was rested even though I had little sleep. I got up and pulled on the thick cloth that opened the metal shutter and let in the full power of the sun. My room instantly filled with life and warmth as

I unlocked the window and opened it letting the scent fill my stuffy bedroom. The neighbour to my Aunt owned a small store she ran from her home. I would soon see that every street in the village had at least one, if not several, tiny home-based stores that supplied the people with necessities as well as pleasures like cold beer. I heard the voices of several men discussing the attacks on neighbouring cities and towns like Vukovar and Vinkovci. I sat back on my bed and listened as they spoke of war and how many had been wounded and killed through the night. I felt embarrassed of my reaction the night before. I was so afraid and felt myself in such a panic, yet, there were people actually being killed while I worried as my bed simply shook. No wonder my Aunt seemed somewhat happy to say it was far away. She knew far better than I of how others were trying to survive the night, much less deal with the discomfort and fear of the what if...

After I reached the kitchen, my Aunt offered me a coffee with some eggs and ham. I gladly accepted and filled my tummy and rid myself of some nerves left over from the night. She didn't mention my question or the fact that I entered her room in the middle of the night. It seemed as though it never happened and so, I chose to follow her lead and leave it alone. After some casual conversation and letting her know how everyone back in Canada had been doing, I decided to go outside and warm up in the sun.

As I opened the big iron gate, I knew I would have to encounter people I didn't know and have yet to meet. I knew I'd see some of my cousins I had just met the day before. I knew I'd struggle with my Croatian in order to keep in conversation and not be a muted bystander. But I felt ready to see what they all looked like, acted like and wanted to say. How would they act toward me? Would they accept me or exclude me? I was ready to find out on my own, without someone by my side. I was the only stranger in this village, and everyone seemed to already know I existed.

I stepped onto the sidewalk and to the left, where our neighbour's store was, there stood a group of four men. Each had an open beer in hand and although just moments ago they had been busy discussing war and death, they suddenly stopped and turned to look at me. I stood still for a moment and stared back at each of them, wondering if I should simply turn back around and go back to my room. Then with a simple tilt of his head and a toothy grin, an older man with streaks of grey scattered through his black, wavy hair, motioned me to join them.

"Good morning our little one from Canada," he smiled. I relaxed myself a bit and walked over to where they stood. "How did you sleep?" Before I could answer, all four men began to laugh.

"Did you enjoy the thunder?" One chuckled. "Or possibly the earthquake?

Did you feel it?" again, laughter. I was confused at that point. Were they joking with me because they felt comfortable with me? Or were they poking fun at me and proving a point of how I simply wouldn't fit in here?

After standing in silence as they laughed and seemed to ask endless silly questions, I cleared my throat and interrupted. "Actually, I was terrified." The words just came without my control. Why did I say that? Their laughter stopped almost instantly. They now stood staring at me without a word and I felt uncomfortable, to say the least. Now what? I thought. I had no idea what to do or say next, so I simply did what I had always known worked in the past. I smiled.

With the simplicity of a smile, came smiles in return. Not laughter, but smiles. I saw through their expression that they understood and somehow, they managed to transform themselves from loud and crude to soft and compassionate.

"That would be a good way of saying it", a middle-aged man said while nodding his head. The others nodded along with him and the discussion now began to take on a new life. I took a seat behind them on a bench secured in front of the store, and one man followed and sat by me. The other two sat on a stone wall only 3 feet tall across from the bench. Soon after, 2 ladies from further up the road came slowly walking toward us and they too, took a seat with our group. Within the next hour, we had at least 15 people hanging out in front of the little community store, discussing everything from the war, to Canada and the worth of a dollar. I made every attempt to stay in the conversation, regardless of which one. I needed to be part of it and the only way these people would accept that I was here, would be to show them I can be there, and want to be with them.

Throughout the day I met new people and people I heard I met before but couldn't remember meeting as I was just a child. My Mom had taken us four siblings to Ivankovo when I was only four years old. A lot of the older folk remembered me, but I didn't remember them. Although I had some faint memories, for the most part, I really didn't know anyone. I heard stories of my parents when they were my age and really enjoyed listening to how life had once been for them. I was able to sit back and enjoy being a part of this small village's life while learning and listening to everyone so eager to share their thoughts and words. It seemed to all be going quite well and I was finding a comfort within this small group gathered by the store. Darla, the store owner, her husband Tom and their two daughters lived in one of the most extravagant homes in Ivankovo and I felt a part of their little world within the afternoon. Sandy, their youngest daughter, was only about a year younger than me and Sindi, about two years my senior.

Sindi was soon to marry my cousin Tomi. They were expecting their first child and decided to marry before the baby was born. So, in this little village where I sat among strangers soon to become my friends and family, life was moving along regardless of the war. People gathered and conversed over beers and coffees, weddings were being planned, and soon I would learn that although nightlife here did not exist due to the ongoing war, towns further west of us still offered discos and life after dark fell. The grumbles of the night before were not even a thought that afternoon. I laughed and others laughed, especially at my broken language. It was far better than I had hoped it would be and I was beginning to feel accepted. Perhaps I really did choose the right path in life for once?

Sandy just finished her shift and came out from the store. Her cousin Zak followed behind her. I had only met her for a short time when I first arrived, but we seemed to click pretty well right away. She ran up and right into my ear whispered with excitement, "Let's go!" They both laughed as they ran off toward his car and I found myself running right behind them. We jumped into his tiny mobile and as he revved his engine and sped away from the gathering, they continued to show great excitement.

"Where are we going?" I asked.

They laughed and responded quickly, "Vinkovci!" Vinkovci was a city approximately 10 km from Ivankovo. It was on one of the front lines and was attacked frequently both by air and land. I knew I was told by others not to go there as it was far too dangerous and unstable. But here I was, being whisked away in a tiny car by two people I barely knew, heading right for the danger zone.

"Where?" I asked. "Did you say Vinkovci?" They once again laughed and continued to speed up the road with one right turn and off to the highway.

Our trip there was short and full of images that would be in my mind forever. I had no time to bring my camera but I knew that nothing, even in photos, would compare to the memory of really seeing these buildings and homes that seemed isolated and forgotten. A lot of rubble. Some of the streets they drove me to were filled with broken stone. Huge holes in houses, buildings, rock and brick scattered within the dusty ruins. I saw only a handful of people walking the streets and even they seemed to be moving in slow motion. It felt completely like another world, it was another world. Within only a few short kilometers from where I was to stay for the next few months, was a city under siege.

"They won't take this one though!" Zak said firmly. "Never." He took one more drive up through a few more streets and passed by the local Hospital. The Hospital itself had enormous holes on every end of it and huge signs asking people to keep away. Everything was quiet.

When we drove back to Ivankovo, they took me to a local cafe and bought me a coffee and cola. We sat for about an hour when we were asked to leave. The owner was closing for the day to avoid any unexpected attacks. We paid our dues and left, still talking about what I had seen for the first time...a city called Vinkovci. Zak drove us home and left. Sandy said she'd be by later to see if I'd like to go to a disco with her and some friends later that evening. She said they knew of one that would be open, about 30 km away. I was happy to have met her and knew she would introduce me to many interesting and most likely, risky places. I waved and went to my Aunt's huge iron gate.

As I opened the gate, I stopped directly in front of my cousin Tomi. I found it quite strange to find him seated in the middle of the yard, on top of what appeared to be my suitcases.

"What are you doing?" I asked him.

"You need to go." He said. "You need to leave here. Tonight. Things are only going to get worse and there's no reason for you to be here. You have to leave." He got up and picked one of my heavier suitcases up from the cold ground. "I'll drive you to the train."

I shook my head and my heart began to race. "No." I replied. "I'm not leaving." We sat and discussed options and scenarios. He stressed that I didn't belong and that I shouldn't put my life in jeopardy. He believed I wasn't thinking and that because I was young, I thought I would live forever.

"You could die here", he said.

"Say what you want, and I understand what you say, but I'm not leaving. Trust me, you aren't responsible for me. My parents know that, I know that. I'm here because I choose to be, I understand that upsets a lot of people. But I'm staying." Although he refused my position for quite a while, he finally sat back down and began to then explain the 'rules of life in this war'. I sat with him and listened intently. I had no idea what these rules could be but I knew they could very well be lifesaving.

Above Photo: Photo of a Post Card by Martin Grgurovac

3 PART THREE
1992 IVANKOVO, CROATIA
LIFE EXPERIENCES AND LESSONS LEARNED

Tomi began by explaining how to walk on the safe side of the street.

"From where we sit," he opened both hands to show the ground we sat on," we wouldn't be safe. When you leave here to go to the center of town, let's say, always walk on the right side of the street going toward the center, then on the same side while returning from the center."

Leaving my Aunt's house, I would have to go right, which was North, in order to reach the center of Ivankovo where most of the cafes were located. The reason, he explained, this side would be the safest was because the attacks would be coming from the East and some from the North, yet none from the South or West. In other words, a rocket flying toward me would sooner either hit the house to my right and shelter me or go past me and I'd be better sheltered once again. Walking on the left would leave me an open target with no shelter of any kind.

"So it's as basic as there are only two possible directions these bombs could come crashing down and by walking on the more sheltered side of the street, the side from which they'd be flying in from, I'd be protected if I was caught in the middle of an attack?" I asked. He nodded and smiled, I was learning quickly.

"Now, if you're already in a house or cafe while there's an attack, then the first place to run would be the underground shelter or basement." He paused and looked up toward the iron gate. "Aunt Kate doesn't have one, but the people across the street in that large house there, " he said pointing above the gate, "they have one and so do I. Though mine's quite small in comparison."

"So, what if there's no shelter?" I asked, knowing there would be more like my Aunt who had no underground hideout.

"Then it's the same as walking on the street. Make sure you're on the lowest level and count the walls." He went on to explain that from the North and East side of Ivankovo, I was to make sure there were the greatest number of walls between those areas and myself. "Once you know you're in the farthest corner away from the North and East, snug yourself right up into that corner and don't move." I closed my eyes and envisioned myself in my Aunt's house. My room faced the street, which faced West.

"So, the safest place in Aunt Kate's house would be my bedroom?" I asked.

"Well, yes and no. The safest place would most likely be the bathroom in the middle of her house. Her house is quite different from most others around here. Hers is quite long and narrow. So with that in mind, the middle of the house would actually be safest. You'll figure it out soon enough," he smiled.

Would I figure it out? I asked myself. Seemed somewhat confusing and I worried that if it didn't already make 100% sense, would it in the midst of an attack? I suppose the best I could do is listen and try to remember every bit he spoke to me.

He shrugged his shoulders and sighed, "then again, if it's your time to go, nothing's going to matter. It'll all be done before you even look up." We sat silent for just a moment.

"I'll be ok now," I smiled, "thank you for explaining it all to me". I hugged him and squeezed my hands then rejoiced, "You have a wedding to plan!" He laughed and nodded. I jumped up and realized my limbs had stiffened, so I bent down quickly to relieve some joint pain. "I forget I'm not twelve sometimes." We laughed and began to walk toward the gate.

"Life goes on, you'll see that around here. War or no war, we have to live. We'll be married soon and then soon after that, we'll have our first baby. Soon after that, well, who knows." He smiled and left the yard as I stood smiling, looking all around me and embracing everything from the stone, the iron gate and the long, narrow yard. I breathed deeply, soaking in every bit of that scent that filled the air so beautifully. Another day had almost come and gone and I turned to pick up my suitcases and return them to my room.

Days passed and life went along with little interruption. Attacks were launched daily on the neighbouring cities of Vinkovci and Vukovar while only a few stray explosions could be felt in Ivankovo. Against my advice and the advice of my Uncle, Aunts, parents and cousins, my Grandparents on my Mother's side returned from their refugee status in Germany. It was only weeks before their return that I had met them in a small town called Tuttlingen in Germany where my Aunt, one of my Mom's sisters, and her 5 children lived.

My Grandparents and my Uncle fled Croatia after the war's onset and sought refuge in Tuttlingen. They were in their 80's and longed to return home. No one could talk them into staying in Germany and they returned to their tiny little stone house just up the street and to the right of where I was staying.

I began my day with my usual coffee, ham and eggs. I was in good spirits this fine day and with some money in my pocket and my cigarettes in the other, I left my Aunt's house and went next door to the store.

"I'm going to visit my Baka and Dida", words in Croatian referring to my Grandmother and Grandfather. I was excited to see them and although I wished they had not returned yet, I was happy to be able to walk to their home for a visit. In Canada, we didn't have Grandparents to visit. We heard stories of them and could imagine them but could never simply walk a block or two, as I could on this beautiful sunny day, for a visit.

"I'll take some bananas please" I said to Sandi. She quickly wrapped several large bananas for me and handed them with joy.

"Will you be long?" She asked.

"I don't think so. They must still be tired from their trip back. I'll be back in time for coffee, no worries". We shared a few laughs and I was off to visit my Grandparents. As I walked up the narrow road, I stayed close along the right side and paid close attention to the houses. I said my greetings to those who sat along the sidewalk on benches and on their front steps, adding a few words to some, then kept going until I reached my first corner. I crossed the street then walked along the North side of the road in order to be blocked and sheltered as instructed. I hoped they liked bananas.

Just as I approached the second house from their tiny home, everything in my bright world changed within a flash. The sound was deafening. One, two, there were four in that first round. I froze for just seconds and stared up to my right. Just above the houses across the street, four rockets pierced through the air and nosedived some place along the intersection I had just passed a moment ago. With no time to waste, I ran straight for my Grandparent's home and slammed the door shut behind me.

My heart raced, my breath short and quick as my pulse ached throughout my body. I struggled to get a hold of myself and found myself facing my Grandparents and Uncle, staring back at me with the same expression I had. We all seemed numb and frozen in time.

"Stand in a corner!" I demanded of them. "*Now!*" My Uncle jumped into a corner and my Grandparents stood still, staring back at me. "You have to move into a corner!" I yelled again. The sounds of the bombs seemed louder and I couldn't figure out where they could be landing. I moved from my corner to grab a hold of my Grandmother's arm. She resisted. She was so small, so fragile, so scared and yet, suddenly so strong.

She looked up at me and pleaded, "I want to go next door to the shelter," she said. I shook my head in disbelief. Tomi never prepared me for this scenario. Although I had wondered how I would remember his 'rules', I had no problem at all remembering every word he spoke. But he never explained what to do or what to say in this situation.

"No," I said as calmly as I could, "we have to stay here. It's not safe out there. There's no protection out there." I pointed to the doorway and tried my best to explain to this wonderful, little old woman that I barely knew, we were to stay put.

She refused and shuffled her way to the door, opened it, then simply walked out. After her, my Grandfather followed. I looked to my Uncle for help but found only a man who shrugged his shoulders. He finally spoke, "you take her, and I'll take him". And so we did.

My Uncle held the arm of my Grandfather and I held the arm of my

Grandmother as we slowly, ever so slowly, walked out of their yard and faced left, directly East, toward her neighbour's home with the shelter. It must have been the longest walk of my life. My Grandmother was old and fragile and even at her most motivated time, walked with steps only inches apart from each other. We walked as rockets were flying by. We walked and thoughts raced through my mind. We walked and I stopped looking toward the skies. I faced down, staring at her feet shuffling over the cracks of the cement. I heard everything, wanted to see nothing.

As we stepped through the iron gate of her neighbour's home, my Uncle quickly reached down and pulled a door from the ground open. Once again, my Uncle and I helped both my Grandparents slowly, very slowly, walk down the cement steps into a dungeon like room. As soon as we had all entered, I pulled the door toward me forcing it closed, blocking out the sun and muffling the sounds of the attack. We were greeted quietly by an older lady, much like my Grandmother and who I thought to be her daughter, and baby granddaughter. A baby. So innocent and so helpless. What a beautiful Mom she had, I thought, to carry her safely down into this dark, cold and damp shelter.

It only took a few short minutes after we seated ourselves to notice the attack had ceased. We were silent, sitting as a group, but silent. When we began to realize that outside fell silent as well, we looked around as though unafraid any longer to view our surroundings.

"I think they stopped", the older lady whispered.

"Yes," my Uncle replied, "I think they did".

My Grandparents sat silent. We waited patiently for another hour and held several short conversations about what each had heard of certain other villages and attacks. Nothing was overstated. Everyone kept their stories short and with little detail. Enough to simply talk, yet not fully acknowledge the very real events outside the walls that sheltered us.

"I brought you bananas, but I can't remember now if I threw them or not," I smiled while my Grandmother smiled in return.

"Thank you," she whispered, "I really like bananas".

Hours later, I began to finally feel suffocated. Outside had been silent and I had the need to get out. I needed to leave and return to my belongings and feel comfort, even though they were simply clothing and little sentimental keepsakes I had brought, I needed to go. My Grandparents begged me to stay. They explained that they would sleep there through the night. I offered to call Germany, and have it arranged that they return to my Aunt's home there, but they refused.

"We need to be home. This place is our home." They said.

I accepted what they spoke and said my goodbyes. I knew they would be safe down in the shelter and felt I had to leave. I hugged each of them, including the older lady, her daughter and gave a kiss to the Grandbaby, then left. The bright sun hurt my eyes only for seconds as I opened the wooden door above me. I closed it quickly and hurried my way down the street. As I approached the intersection, I noticed a man standing on a rooftop with what seemed to be a hammer and some sheets of wood. I ran quickly, on the guarded side of the street, and reached for the large gate to my Aunt's house.

"Lucy!" a shout startled me and I jumped back at least a few feet. "Lucy!" again came the sound of a voice full of relief. It was Sandi, my neighbour. She ran and hugged me as though we had been long lost friends from years gone by. "Thank God you're ok!" Before I could even respond, a crowd gathered around me which included my cousin and two Aunts along with some neighbours. I had hugs from each of them and blessings were shared throughout the group that gathered outside my gate.

"You just left when it all started!" Sandi exclaimed.

"I know!" I laughed. "I was almost at Baka's house when I saw the first four fly by!" My eyes widened as I spoke of the experience. We sat on the bench, some on the stone steps, others stood, as we spoke of the day and what I had done with my Grandparents. Everyone shared a bit of their own story and feelings, then came the news of those who suffered.

"He's deaf, mute. He couldn't hear them and well," the man paused, "he's alive, but is now missing both his legs. He was on the road when they landed and the shrapnel got him badly on the lower half." He was the only casualty in Ivankovo that day while several homes were hit. The man on the roof I had seen, he had one land through his rooftop.

"But I saw him up there, he looked like he was fixing something," I said.

"Yes, he was fixing the big hole the rocket left behind!" A woman shouted to me. "What do you think? We're messy people? If there's a big hole in our roof, we fix it!"

Then a man jumped in, "Yes! And if they bomb again and make another hole, we fix it again! We do it every day when we have to!" It was a pride among them. Sadness was definitely present but so was this unexpected zest for life. They seemed somewhat energized explaining to me of how life was to be lived. We couldn't let evil destroy us. We would move on.

4 PART FOUR
1992 IVANKOVO, CROATIA
LIFE CONTINUES EVEN IN WAR

I was uncomfortable here, not really knowing anyone. Invited to a wedding in such a small village was definitely an experience I needed to go through. Sandi, although I had only met her a short time ago, was by my side through most of the day with her informal introductions as people passed by. Curiosity brought most toward our table, while others whispered amongst each other looking at me from a short distance. Life in a village, especially during a war, rarely brought a new face for them to encounter. Yet, there I was, sitting, smiling, waiting for the day to end as others looked on questioning my presence.

"*What in the name of God are you doing here??*" That was a question I heard all too often after meeting yet another resident of this tiny place. I made every attempt to be unique with my response to this popular query. "Just popped by for a visit", "this trip is my Grad present", "I'm a little nuts"..... Whatever my answer, I seemed to bring a smile to the faces filled with worry and at times, anger. I understood all too well how I was able to infuriate most who lived here. All who could escape this place, whether by refugee status or illegally, left long ago. Those who remained, were literally stuck with no way out. And there I was, an 18 year old Canadian girl with a Passport to freedom and luxury, seated at a wedding among trapped souls who felt their only fate was to die in this war. I seemed nothing more than a smiling idiot who wanted to flash my freedom card to those suffering. Definitely not true, but to most of them, truth didn't much matter anymore.

Sandi sat to my left and giggled with a guy I had myself recently met. I smiled, acting as though I too was participating in their conversation, but didn't hear a word. I slowly looked around wondering what these people were feeling, thinking or dreaming of. Since my arrival, just a few short weeks ago, I had been overcome by a need to know what they had been through, felt and lived like each day. *How did the war affect them? What was lifelike during a war? What, if any, hopes and dreams do they have now?* I could only imagine what I might learn and was excited to go on that journey.

A couple stood by the large iron gate ten feet to my left while drinking what looked to be red wine. The woman wasn't smiling while the man seemed to make an attempt to coax her into happiness. To their right, an elderly woman wore a black cotton dress, black apron and a matching handkerchief wrapped over her hair. She sat on a wooden chair at the corner where the stone house and iron gate joined. A group of children played by the chicken coup toward the back side of the yard. I was quite absorbed in the scene around me and hadn't noticed Sandi calling to me.

"What's wrong with you?" she asked.

"Nothing," I replied, "I was just thinking". Most times I found that by smiling, or even laughing at the end of anything I ever said, helped ease others and bring them back to happy times. So instead of dealing with an endless explanation of where my thoughts had been, I smiled and chuckled to avoid some in depth conversation as to why I hadn't heard her call to me from shoulder's length. As predicted, she turned her back and continued talking to her friend, forgetting she ever even called to me in the first place. Worked like a charm.

It was then that I noticed him. Seated directly in front of me with his long, bony fingers spread like a fan over his face. He seemed a very timid, yet somewhat eerie looking guy. His hair was a mousy brown and his eyes, from what I could see of them peeking through his hands, were a darker brown. I was sure he caught my stare but in an instant, his head turned to his right then bowed down toward the ground.

I shifted my attention quickly so I wouldn't offend this strange fellow with such an intense reaction to my attention and joined in Sandi's conversation. Everyone was eager to celebrate the day with both Bride and Groom. The Groom, my first cousin, was about to marry his next door neighbour Sindi and commit to a life of love and joy, or so we hoped. She was now about 6 months pregnant and as far as both families were concerned, there was no time to waste. War, as far as I had learned, never could put an absolute silence and finality to their lives. At least not in the unoccupied zones. If a wedding was to be, it would be, regardless of the always present enemy just miles away. I only heard a handful of guests mention a possible air attack that day, but no one gave it more than the mere mention and all was left alone.

"Sandi", I whispered as she readied herself for the ceremony.

"What is it?" she asked. "I have to go help Sindi with her gown soon."

"I just wanted to know about the one guy who sat across from us earlier," I continued, "do you know him?"

She finished tucking a loose strand of hair back into place and turned toward me. "Oh, no, you can't talk to him. In fact," she went on, "even if you tried to, he wouldn't talk to you. He hasn't even said much to his own Mother about his battles here." She stopped and looked to me as though waiting for my reassurance and promises to keep away. I said nothing. She turned and finished touching up her lip gloss and said, "all I do know is that he was the one who destroyed the very first enemy tank in this war, and he hasn't said anything to anyone since. There's a lot of talk, even that he's lost it completely, not that I believe it but that's the rumor. You must stay away from him, he's just not safe."

"Ok," I muttered and walked toward the door before she could go on with her warnings and orders. As I was about to leave, I stopped and asked, "what's his name?"

She huffed as though irritated at a child with a million questions and grunted, "Milan." Satisfied, I left the room and waited for the day to end, knowing I just might get some sleep that night.

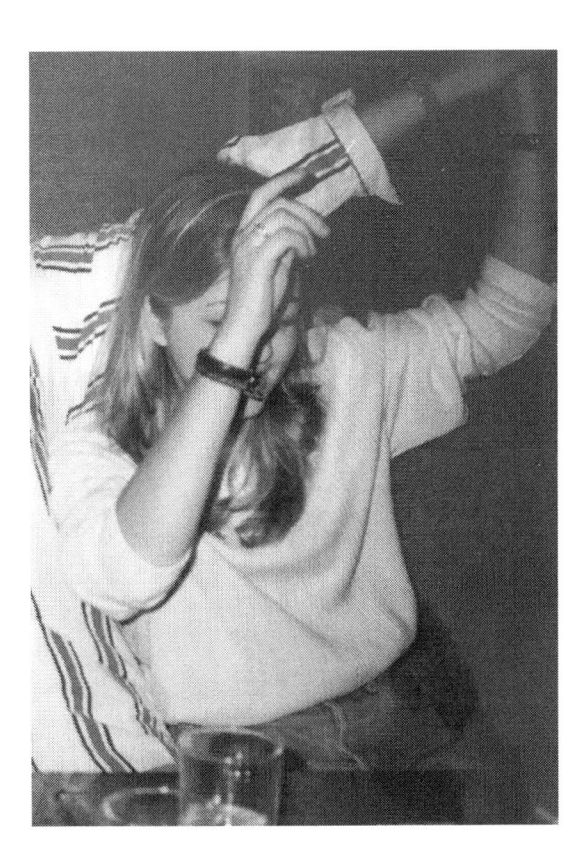

*Center of Ivankovo, Croatia.
Small concrete wall to the right is where we would sit and talk.*

5 PART FIVE
1992 IVANKOVO, CROATIA
MEETING MILAN

It was late, I'd say close to 8:30 at night. With the way things had been since my arrival, to be in the center of Ivankovo past 8:00pm was almost equal to an all nighter back home. Nightfall was about to take over the beautiful sky and sirens could soon boom over the rooftops. Sandi called to me as she said goodnight to the group we just finished chatting with. The cafe's closed early during the war and with that, it left nothing for us to do but go home and occasionally play cards by candlelight. Just another evening out to try and socialize for an hour or two, then walk down the street to our rooms and try to sleep.

I waved goodbye to the group and turned to join her for our walk, when I noticed a man seated on the two foot high concrete wall that lined the road by the intersection. There, at the very corner, he sat alone. I recognized him right away. His back was bent with his head cowering toward the ground, hand fanned directly over his face, totally alone. It was Milan. A week had passed since the wedding and I had never seen him there in the center before. In fact, I had no idea he lived in this village as he never came to any of the cafes since my arrival. I was more than curious to learn what brought him to this corner, at this time of night, when all were just leaving for the safety of their homes.

"You're not staying!" Sandi insisted as she noticed I stopped, staring in Milan's direction.

"Oh," I began as I looked directly into her eyes, "yes I am." I was ready to meet any challenge or protest she may throw at me and she knew it well from my eyes and my stance.

"Fine," she quickly retreated, "but I'm going home." She began to walk away and added, "I'm not responsible for anything that happens after I leave, so good luck." She rushed off in anger and disappeared around the corner within seconds.

And there I stood, totally alone in the center of this village with a man apparently feared by most just twenty feet away. What was I thinking? I knew I could run and I knew I could scream, but I also knew there was nothing to fear. I was ready to meet Milan and I hoped I was ready for anything he wanted to say. When Sandi vanished and the street was silent, Milan slowly lifted his head and moved his hand from his face. When his eyes looked directly at mine, I knew, he had come to see me. What I didn't know at that time, was that this would be the first of many, many meetings to come.

Although I stood motionless for what seemed forever, I slowly moved toward him, still watching one another with no words spoken. I stopped just short of two feet from where he sat and waited for a sense of what I should do next. He placed both hands behind him and straightened out his back ever so slowly, then hunched over instantly as though being pulled by an elastic. His eyes still looking to mine.

"I'm Milan," he whispered. I smiled as a chuckle escaped my throat and said, "I know," then followed with, "I'm Lucy." He smiled awkwardly and said, "I know."

I sat beside him on the concrete wall and breathed in the sweet scent I loved so much, enjoyed the pure silence of the night, and waited for whatever was going to happen that night. He seemed, for a minute, to regret coming. He nervously twisted his fingers together then whispered, "I saw you at the wedding."

"Yeah," I replied quickly with intent to keep the conversation going, "I saw you too." I waited only a few seconds before adding, "I asked about you, that's how I know your name."

"I asked about you too," he said. We both smiled, knowing that we had just overcome a large part of what had once felt so awkward. "I would have talked to you, but" he paused, "there were a lot of people there. Most of them would have had too many questions if they saw us talking. Everyone knows who you are, even if you don't know them. They watch everything you do and everyone you're with." I nodded and fully understood that what he said was true. The guests at the wedding would have had far too much to imagine had they seen the two of us talking. They watched every move I made and whispered with every action or word I spoke to anyone. As far as I understood, they did the same with Milan. Milan would have been an even greater topic for them to whisper about, especially considering he didn't talk to anyone, even his own Mother.

"I heard you don't talk a lot anyway," I said.

"Not really, I don't like everyone talking about me, it makes me feel uncomfortable. When I don't talk, they have much less to say. They all think they know something, when in reality, they know nothing." He stopped and stared at my eyes and said, "they think I'm crazy."

I smiled and without even so much as a blink, I said "Yeah, they really do." And with that, our friendship began. He was an amazing person and I was honored to have not only met him but develop a true friendship that would continue for months to come. That night, we sat on the concrete walls for hours, talking as though we had so much to catch up on with so little time. Soon after our first words were spoken, he held the concrete wall with his hands instead of hiding behind them. His one leg often swung out then rocked back playfully as he spoke with words that kept my mind racing with images he created so vividly. He admitted that the things he had told me, he in fact had never told even his own Mother. He couldn't live knowing she might fear for him, or for his sanity.

"But, everyone already thinks you're unstable," I began, avoiding the use of the term 'crazy' at that point, "why not show them this side of you? Then, maybe they might not worry or talk about you so much anymore."

"It's not that simple," he began. "This way, even though they may say I'm crazy, they really don't know if I am. If I told them some stories, they might really believe I'm crazy and after that, I have no chance." He paused and turned to me, "Understand?"

"Yes." I replied. "That actually makes sense. It's like giving them information to help them understand, only to have them use it and turn it against you." He nodded and smiled, reassured that I was following what he was really trying to explain. I often found myself repeating words to ensure others understood, I understood. My knowledge of the Croatian language sometimes seemed less than it really was.

As he continued with his story of the very first enemy tank to be shot down by his own hands, he stopped abruptly, frozen as though something had just hit him. With a glimmer in his eyes, he turned to me and grinned. "Wait right here!" I watched as he leapt off the wall we made ourselves comfortable on for hours, and within seconds, he was running across the street.

"Where are you going?" I shouted after him.

"I'll be right back! Just wait there!" He shouted back without giving me a chance to respond. He vanished behind a row of trees as I sat stunned and confused. Well, I thought to myself, *this is strange. Has he now lost his mind? Were they all right about him all along? Had I become so naïve as to think I could actually have a conversation with a guy a whole village thought to be insane? Would he come back or would I sit here, all alone, until I'd finally decide to go home? Even worse, would he return to kill me?* With the stories I heard from others, things like that were definitely possible, even with some of the sanest individuals. Although some fear definitely made its way into my heart, I insisted to myself that I would wait it out. I was curious to know how this night would end. He wasn't crazy, I felt it, I knew it.

Finally, the bushes rustled and he emerged with a huge grin holding a rocket launcher, what was called I believed, an 'Osa' on his shoulder. This large and very intimidating weapon was used to destroy tanks. Coming towards me his smile wide, he almost skipped the last few feet until he reached where I sat waiting.

"This is it!" he exclaimed. "This very thing was what I shot the first enemy tank with and I was allowed to keep it. Go ahead! Hold it and see what it feels like!" His excitement to share this with me was contagious and I was thrilled to be invited into this historic moment, hearing his every word and now, so close to holding a weapon that was literally used in such a monumental way. He helped me shoulder it and began telling me of the day he shot this intimidating weapon. He only had one shot. His story was incredible as he began retelling it as though he was in the very spot he had been in that day. I couldn't help but feel as though I had been there myself and felt a panic with his words painting a most terrifying place and time.

I AM Lucy

6 PART SIX
1992 IVANKOVO, CROATIA
LOOKING BACK

Exhausted from a night full of vivid war stories still fresh in the mind of a soldier, I was left questioning mankind and motives of not just governments, soldiers and civilians, but of myself and what I truly felt I was doing in this country and what in the world I thought I would ever accomplish here. Even if I stayed in Zagreb as originally planned, *how would I have really helped? Would anything I could have done there really been helpful to those who lived on the front lines? Those who battled not only mine fields but the demons within them?* I thought back to my last months of High School in Calgary.

1991, My grad year. I was what I liked to call a chronic skipper through high school and although most teachers would have rather had me expelled for my absences, there were some who accepted who I was and encouraged me to continue to attend. My parents didn't understand why I had such a difficult time wanting to attend classes and although they pushed me in every way possible, I battled with attendance through the full three year system. I was more than willing to attend the school itself, but when that awful buzzer rang and everyone herded themselves into one of those confined classrooms and the doors closed, I felt suffocated and as though I was trapped. I wanted to be free. I could pass tests and finish book reports, write essays and achieve high grades even with an awful attendance record. Funny enough, I could do this even without reading the books and still perform an oral report along with a written. The fact I didn't attend daily classes though always put me in a lower grade point average as most teachers felt being present meant something. At the time, I felt the lower grades were worth the bit of freedom I gained.

Passing everything regardless of this, I had a gift I suppose yet this frustrated almost every adult that I encountered. Society in general was to me, frustrating. Probably as frustrating as I was to them. Clock in, clock out, do what you're told, even though the other 29ish students around you each had different traits, abilities and dreams. All were treated the same and were expected to learn the exact same thing, day in and day out. I would much rather open my notebook, sit by my locker and doodle away in peace while others panicked trying to get to class before they were late. This worked for a lot of them. I admired those who didn't even think about the fact they were corralled like livestock and never even understood my comparison as such. I simply couldn't convince myself to understand and accept this as normal, no matter how hard I tried or how hard those around me tried.

Our High School Career Day had been the biggest disappointment for me. Walking into the school where there were a multitude of booths, so many that I simply walked past most without giving them any attention at all. I walked and tried to get a feel of what I could possibly do with my life. Nothing. I watched as those I knew very well had ambitions and goals to attain, racing toward specific booths and with excitement, began filling forms and having discussions with those so similar to themselves. I felt nothing walking past the University booths offering too many options to even be bothered with. I walked past each booth and watched the smiles of those trying to entice students to become part of their missions. Selected members of higher education, inviting these kids to focus on their goals and sign over their long-term commitment to ensure debt for years and a lifetime of paying taxes, in exchange for high paying careers, drawing in many for the sign off.

All I really saw were the faces of scholars who had little hope anyone from our school would actually succeed. I was positive these people weren't really there to sign us all up, but to show us who and what we couldn't be. Statistically, the Forest Lawn area of Calgary was not known for a high ratio of studious and successful Doctors and Lawyers and I had to chuckle at the responses I received when I finally would stop at a couple of the stands. They lost interest in me within the first two questions. Little did they know that one day, my dream was to be a Psychologist and yet all they did was judge me, leaving me with such a poor impression of the educated elite.

Would it have really been all that difficult for at least one of them to be open minded and discuss options with me? Why they wouldn't send mascots who could motivate and encourage youth was beyond me. People who seemed happy would have been helpful, not those who had practiced their smiles before a mirror that morning, rehearsing their monologues and promises of a brighter future.

Ready to head out from the overwhelming judgment of those assigned to be there this day, those who had come to entice new recruits, I finally saw what I felt could be the answer to my own future and felt I actually had a career, for the time being, to which I was willing to sign my life away. I wished to change the world for at least a year before committing myself to a degree. With excitement, I quickly walked to the booth with the large lettered banner reading "Become a Missionary". I scanned the pamphlets they had, the photographs they printed and the brochures and saw nothing but poor, helpless people of this world in need of someone, anyone to help. I saw as they were helped by way of food, clothing, building shelters and homes and I was certain, even though I always had a dislike for the silliness of our school system, I would be able to help those in need to even learn skills they could use to improve their lives. I felt an enormous relief and excitement with this wonderful option! Why hadn't I ever thought of this myself? Maybe this career fair wasn't so silly after all and truly gave some hope for our futures.

As the woman with her hands lightly clasped together watched me soak in all the information, she patiently waited for me to notice her. Before she could say a word, I rushed with excitement and asked her to sign me up immediately and explained I was ready and able to leave at any time. I told her I would go anywhere in the world and only needed a small space to sleep, could sleep on a floor, ate very little and needed no pay at all. I was so eager to begin this journey that I could hardly contain my excitement! This was such a new feeling that I surprised myself as I had no idea I even had this amazing ability to look forward to the future. With all of these visions racing through my mind I realized the woman was still so calm, collected and well, slow to react.

I waited for her to direct me to some sort of sign up page or offer me a business card when she finally said in her gentle tone, "That's wonderful! Once you finish a degree, please come see us and we will be happy to sign you up!" And just like that, my life became the Road Runner show. I was

Wylie E Coyote and a huge boulder just dropped on my head while society once again laughed, squealed a '*beep-beep*' and ran away with my dreams.

She continued, "any Degree will do. A teacher, a nurse, it really doesn't matter but once you've completed that, we can get you started on your way to helping the needy." She smiled wide and so pleased with herself, she unclasped her hands and gently clapped them together barely making a sound. I struggled and somehow managed to speak the words, "you're kidding." Without giving her much more time to continue to repeat her rehearsed lines, I left the school and went home with even more disappointment in our world than I had that morning, which even I didn't think possible.

My walk home was quick and although I normally enjoyed my walk past the neighbourhood I knew like the back of my hand, I barely noticed anything until I was finally seated on the couch at home. I turned the TV on to see what was on the 3 channels we had and sulked in my misery yet again trying to figure out what I would do with my life. Hours passed and the news began and as always, I sat intently watching the news of the world, believing every word they spewed to me through the box and watched as they played footage of the evils in the world in which we lived. And that's when it all came to me.

War in what was known as Yugoslavia broke out this year, 1991, and according to our local newscaster, whom I trusted daily for years, the aggressor was unknown as there were too many parties involved. They detailed that although war was definitely raging, they didn't know if it was the Croats, the Serbs or the Bosnians who were the actual aggressors. They had no idea and therefore, they couldn't send help and the UN refused to enter into such an unknown state of war. Confusing to say the least but I understood this to be true at the time. The footage they showed also wasn't all too terrible. There were scenes of rubble and some older people walking slowly through the crumbled stones, seeming to search for missing items. It really didn't seem all that drastic and was unlike what I had heard of previous wars this world had seen. She didn't announce any death tolls or news of wounded. For now, the world could only sit and wait to be able to better determine who the actual aggressor was and, in the meantime, they would send aid via shipments and potential volunteers to certain areas and continue to request cease fires from all warring sides.

With that and as simple as it seemed, I made my decision to go to Croatia. My decision was literally made within the small news clip and was, in my opinion, my only choice. I somewhat knew the language. I had relatives there, even though I had never met most of them. I could reach the capital, Zagreb, and offer myself to help in any way possible. I had two friends who had already gone to do this and thought this was the perfect opportunity for me to make a difference in this world we all lived in. I wouldn't need to make any arrangements other than to convince my parents to support my decision to go. Little did I know that after a few weeks and finally winning the debate with my parents and having their blessing to go, then after flying to Germany to be driven into Croatia where I would begin my new life of helping those in need and making a difference in the world, and after reaching my destination of Zagreb, Croatia, my friends weren't there and the contacts I had, all left Zagreb and no one had any idea when they would return.

And that, in a nutshell, was how I ended up not only going to Croatia, but then leaving Zagreb to enter some front lines. Osijek, Croatia was my first front line.

7 PART SEVEN
1992 IVANKOVO, CROATIA
I NEVER WANTED TO LEAVE

Since my arrival, I battled through the culture shock of seeing soldiers everywhere, carrying guns as though they were simply school kids carrying backpacks on their way to school. I changed my sightseeing behaviors when stepping off a train and being surrounded by pure destruction and giant, gaping holes in buildings, seeking immediate shelter instead of reaching for my camera. I stopped judging those who appeared to simply be drunk and babbling to themselves and realized, most were sober victims of the most horrific experiences many would never be able to imagine surviving, much less continue to find a way to keep living. So many stories that one day I would dream of writing in detail while for now, I eagerly scribbled notes in journals I kept under my pillow. Even here in Ivankovo, my Mom made sure I always had notebooks so I would never stop writing. The mailman would bring me my new supply all the way from Canada and I was never without my pen and journals, always scribbling my days into the night.

Arriving in Croatia near the end of February of 1992, I had a plan. I had a plan and believed that plan would help me become part of what society had always wanted and expected of me. To have plans, set goals, move toward them and stick to them. Be responsible and become an adult with purpose. By the end of July 1992, I realized my plan, my goal and my efforts to bring them to life with purpose were futile. It was midnight and everyone was fast asleep while I embraced the rare silence and peaceful calm in the air. As I sat on the coolness of the concrete mini wall just outside my neighbor's store, the burning heat of the sun now gone yet the air still surrounding me with comforting heat. As I breathed in the scent I had already forgotten was once foreign yet so inviting to me, I watched the obsidian like sky in the distance flash with brilliant white light lasting minutes each time. The white light was an absolute contrast to the darkness which it invaded as the night ever so slowly crept away. Such beauty, such devastation.

As I watched a hemisphere shine so bright one would think a million candles were suddenly lit, then extinguished, tears slowly trickled down my cheeks as I made no sound and continued to keep my breath hushed. Each glow, each brilliant shine, brought more death and disaster. I sat, watching a war from afar as Bosna and Hercegovina was under siege. This is what it looks like, I thought, to watch people die from a distance and do nothing to stop it.

While war was still a constant here, another had begun and I wondered what the news was relaying to my friends back at home. I shook my head thinking how they were being told, yet again; still no full understanding of what this war was about, no idea who the aggressor was, they couldn't help until they had full cooperation and cease fires… I wondered if those watching the box I used to so intently watch, and those listening closely to the words I once listened so closely to, knew that I sat here now angry with the world for their constant interference within this country? Although I once believed the world could help stop a war, I learned that the world simply helped increase the fight and energy of a war. There were too many ways to think of then, but I knew I would struggle to forgive the world for it all, if ever I could forgive it that is.

Each time the UN announced a new date of arrival, we were attacked daily, nightly and fiercely until that date arrived. During these attacks, our own Government of course would insist we follow the order of cease fire leaving us sitting ducks, just waiting for the next rocket to land, next bullet to pierce, next mig to drop devastation. Then, of course, because there had been no cease fire and even though it was only due to the aggressor, I had to listen as the UN announced that, 'due to heavy attacks and no cease fire, they would not be sending their troops until'…. Yet another new date which equaled another series of attacks upon the people of this war-torn country. I wished the UN would just shut up and leave everyone alone! I wished the world would ignore us instead of lie about us! I wished this Country would simply unleash a full-blown attack on the aggressors and that this, and only this, would actually end the war and any further loss and devastation.

I wished I hadn't stayed long enough to see those blue helmets of the UN that I had grown to associate with devastation, finally arrive. I wished I didn't see, firsthand, the embargoes they placed on the aggressor publicly, yet privately, I watched as their cargo vans and trucks loaded with supplies quietly snuck through the barricades and supplied the aggressors through the darkness of the night. They didn't know I was with soldiers during night watch, sitting in the midst of those protecting me, only to watch those from the world taking steps to make that job to protect me and the civilians of this country, that much more impossible for them to do. They didn't care that the soldiers saw them. They didn't even look our way, knowing we were there, they truly didn't care. I grew even angrier thinking of General Mackenzie and wished I had news cameras with me to show everyone what he and his little crew were really doing there. I struggled to release the anger and return myself to breathe slowly, stay hushed and focused on living. Focused on not taking for granted that I still sat on the coolness of the mini wall in peace, for now.

Far away from here. I thought back to my very first night in Ivankovo and recalled the trembling of the bed I lied in. My thoughts brought me back to my panic and my Aunt's calm, almost humorous reaction to my intrusion of her bedroom and sleep. Be grateful. Be thankful. It's far away from here. My tears grew thicker still and although they now raced to fall from my cheeks, I continued to hush myself. I controlled my breathing and sat still, watching the skies explode then fade away into black. *I should be grateful*, I thought. *I should be thankful*, I thought. But as much as I desperately wanted to feel grateful and thankful, I couldn't even remember what those had ever even felt like. *How was it that only 5 months ago I accepted this great gift of privilege that I had of being safer than those in neighboring towns and cities just kilometers away? How could I have ever thought that simply being present, being with these people was better than those who stayed away and that I was at least doing something and being a part of something? When had I become a person who was content with just sitting, alone, in a war-torn country surrounded by more war-torn countries, just watching?*

This night evolved from my simple motivation of enjoying a beautiful, calm and quiet summer night in a country with people who had welcomed me into their lives, and I simply wanted to sit and appreciate all that I had lived, learned and survived. At first, I felt accomplished and proud. I truly loved these people I met and came to know so well and I understood they were not only survivors and warriors, but they were my best teachers. They taught me how to live and that life has so much more meaning than I ever imagined.

I joined several soldiers through night watch during some of my sleepless nights and we would quietly sit in our position until the rise of dawn. While they silently shared their stories of life which led them to their paths of defending their homes and of what their dreams would be once the war ended, I didn't want to imagine that some, or maybe most, would never fulfil those dreams. I didn't want to imagine it, but I did. I didn't want to know the plans and dreams of many would be taken from them against their will. *All for what? For what?!?* These weren't boys and girls, men and women, who couldn't wait to kill their enemy and lived only to kill then reach their own deaths in battle. They weren't dreaming of the day they would lay, lifeless and bloodied on a battlefield reaching their lifelong dreams of war and death. No. They were people like me, like my friends at home, like those we see rushing to work through rush hour traffic. They were people who had a job to do and they had pride in doing so, while praying for the day they could enjoy peace and get married, have children, travel….

The people of this country showed me how to not take life for granted but to celebrate it instead. Even in the dark of night when the entire village had mandatory lights out and even during enemy attacks and when the sirens sent out their warnings. Even when huddled in the dampness of a cellar while rockets exploded above and even when our friends, sons, fathers and brothers and yes, women as well, were out there somewhere standing their ground to protect us from further harm, being told they weren't allowed to fire back as the world gave this order to them. And, even when old men cried relaying to me their stories of torture and heart break as they were forced to watch as their loved ones were brutally killed! The old men with their eyes held open by enemy soldiers and their bodies forcibly confined so they could not move, even slightly, forced to endure a pain no words would ever be able to fully explain. This, they had no choice but to see, to hear, to watch and feel every agony, every second of the brutal deaths their wife or child suffered before them, just feet away. The immense pain of their helplessness and torment ripped their souls apart, only to be released and told they would be free now, to live with these images for the rest of their days, years, lives. Yes, free. They were set free.

I could imagine hearing the news, men set free following a lengthy attack on the city, they were set *free*. I could imagine the audience listening to the broadcast, feeling relief that these men were set free. What a relief! Freedom! Yes, the audience, regardless of where they were within this world we shared, would be relieved and once again hopeful that there was in fact a possibility for peace after all and that at least some, these men, had been set free. They should be so happy, so grateful, these men somehow set free. The world would never care to ask what this freedom meant to them. What the freedom truly meant. That the cost for their freedom would keep them imprisoned within their minds forever. How free they really were, while never ever would they be, free. I was still told by these very men to appreciate my freedoms and that they truly were happy for me knowing that I would never, ever have to know this pain. Even these people, these who suffered beyond my understanding, never would wish harm on me or those who had never experienced their pain. Even they accepted their fate of reliving torture on their own, not wanting this to happen to anyone else. They taught me about owning my own life and whatever may happen with it. I prayed I would never, ever forget this.

At first, the night skies felt calm and soothing. I reflected on the months passed and surprised even myself with the stories I heard and also the events I lived through firsthand. I had seen rockets many times pierce through the air overhead! I had cowered low behind and even under bushes as enemy aircraft flew low above, heading toward their destinations of destruction! I learned to never fear a rocket you can hear and trained my ears to be able to know the exact time a rocket was launched, which direction it was heading, and how far away it would land! I knew that when I heard a rocket pop at launch, even though this was at least launched from 20km away, if it wasn't followed by the ear-piercing screech of flight, **RUN**!! Left or right! Just run! This is the rocket that's heading directly towards you! I ran many times in the hope of safety down into cellars and waited inside bathrooms centered in homes and even slept inside bathtubs. Sandi and I believed it was just that much extra buffer between us and potential shrapnel. Just like a feather quilt or even a tree. Anything between us and shrapnel was better than nothing. I ran left and right. I ran many times and understood the patterns, sounds and silence as well.

I shook my head and sighed remembering I had even been held hostage at gunpoint on a train once. How I managed to escape when even Sandi, poor Sandi, tried desperately to open and even kicked the locked door repeatedly to the tiny storage room I was locked in, being held captive. I was thankful she stopped kicking as it wasn't helping, only aggravating my captor that much quicker. After trying for hours to plead for my release and after this Officer explained how he could easily throw my body out of the wide yet narrow window as we traveled in the desolate countryside, I realized he was angry not with me, but what and who I represented. I met so many who could forgive what I represented and understood the world didn't owe them a thing, even though I believed they did. I met so many who somehow fought through their demons and stayed in the now and refused to hurt others out of their pain.

This Officer was not an evil man but had seen evil, lived evil and although I would never know what evils tortured him within, I was suddenly the symbol of the evil he knew. He was in a full PTSD episode and although it took me hours to realize it, I already knew him through the many men I met sharing their stories and teaching me how they found the strength to keep living despite their traumas. I escaped with my life by telling this Officer I would no longer be his friend and he had lost my respect. Out of all other methods I tried to use, this was the only thing that truly affected this man who at first, I thought, was simply a crazy person. After my release, I realized just how angry Sandi was and the awful situation she had been in knowing I would never purposely disappear like that. I understood her anger and helplessness. I felt so badly for her, yet managed to make her laugh when I reminded her that it was me who almost died and yet she was trying to steal my thunder. We agreed to never speak of it again, after all, we both made it home safe and sound. I would insist to myself to only learn from the experience and not become traumatized or victim to it. I was that much stronger because of it and more compassionate. Life went on.

So many memories came flooding to me and although at first they brought me pride, the night had brought this ominous light show and with it, an immense feeling of failure. I failed to help others, I thought. I failed to make a difference and I needed to find a way to help. I needed to go home. I had no real purpose, I thought, by staying any longer. My sister was soon to get married and this would be a perfect time to return. I thought I would return to Canada, tell others of all the truths I'd seen myself and witnessed firsthand. I would tell them of real-life stories shared with me and maybe this would help someone, some time, somehow. My tears flowed with force now as dawn was breaking and the white glow in the distance disappeared. I would miss these people terribly. I never wanted to leave but I set myself free. I wished there was a way to make my life here and stay forever, but it was time for me to go.

This is me. Vinkovci, Croatia.

8 PART EIGHT
1992 CALGARY, CANADA
A STRANGER IN MY HOMETOWN

I didn't expect to experience culture shock following my return to Calgary. It surprised me just how quickly I became part of such a different culture overseas in such a short time. Here, there were no soldiers walking the streets and there were no eager eyes trying to meet with mine to see the foreign girl. There were no stories being shared on benches in residential areas and no one to invite me in for a coffee and cookie while we chatted about life in general or the weather. Those with whom I tried to say a friendly hello to while walking down the street darted glares before quickening their steps, rushing away before I could have any opportunity to say any more.

Although I was born here, in the General Hospital in the Bridgeland area of Calgary, raised in Radisson Heights and only moved to the outskirts of the city with my parents after high school, I was completely out of place. Calgary was, until the past 5 months, all I ever really knew yet I realized I didn't even know it at all. Just now, after I returned from Croatia, I started to realize how intense my life had been in Croatia and how much I absorbed during my time there, while an entire lifetime here in Calgary, I knew very little about the people who actually lived here with me or about their lives.

Everywhere I turned I saw multitudes of people just moving about their day, quickly, very quickly. I remembered back to my first walks in Ivankovo when the ladies shouted after me, asking where I was off to in such a hurry. Laughing at me and my odd behavior, these wonderful ladies with whom I became friends within a matter of minutes, were puzzled at my fast pace, yet I had nowhere to go. Taking a walk had become a pleasure and a relaxing break over in the small village, even in a war zone, while here, in Calgary, I saw what I never realized during all my years before. Such a fast pace. A rush. Go, move, keep going, move ahead again until you finally reach the bed at the end of the day, exhausted. Schedule people in to talk and catch up only to hear of how fast their lives had been moving along as well. Very little time to sit, enjoy, dream. I sighed but understood this should be a simple transition and I wouldn't need to rejoin the race, so there was no need to let them affect me. I would continue to live my life as though I was in the small village and walk slowly, enjoy my time and never join the race with no finish line in sight. If I stuck to this plan, I could accomplish creating a piece of the small village atmosphere right here in Calgary. This is what I thought. This was soon, I realized, a silly wish that would never really come to life.

The first few weeks were somewhat a blur. Although I hadn't raced through time, others were unable, or unwilling, to slow themselves down to simply have a discussion or wait for my answers to their questions. I tried to understand their thought patterns. It took several seconds for me to actually understand what their questions were and why they would ask them. I was disappointed because I realized, their questions were never intended to receive true answers. They were almost pre-programmed and answers were to be the same. I took my time to hear their questions so I could answer them truthfully. This wasn't what they wanted. This wasn't what they understood. Their *'how are you'* required an *'I am fine'* and the rest would follow the same pattern. I was not just simply confused, but again, disappointed and wished I could better grasp their mind set. It wasn't as easy as I thought it would be coming back home. I looked at things far differently now. I heard things differently. I even felt things differently. What was once all I ever knew was now all a life I felt I never knew before. It was a life of programming, not a life to be lived each minute. There was no time to allow for the minutes as they were faster here than where I had been.

Even the simplest of things changed. One night just after 11:00pm, the fireworks for the Stampede I had grown up with had become a completely different experience all together. My brother and I were at home watching TV when I jumped, seemingly without reason. As he stared at me wide eyed as though questioning my sanity, I returned his look and remained calm when I questioned him, wondering what the explosions were. I believe at this point he truly felt I had lost my mind. He heard nothing. As I began to narrate to him as the sound of a small rocket was being launched, or what I believed to be some sort of small explosive, I then counted out loud the amount of seconds this explosive whizzed through the air, then I exclaimed the exact point at which this explosive actually exploded, he still looked at me as though I was from another world. I was just as confused as I knew the explosive actually exploded but didn't have impact with anything when it did. The direction was also just as puzzling and I was quickly becoming concerned. I hadn't heard this type of explosion before, yet it was definitely happening. I turned the TV off and he still couldn't hear what I heard, now even louder for only me. It was then that we both insisted we investigate this as I was absolutely shocked he couldn't hear these and feared for our safety, and he believed I was most likely just a little crazy.

It took no time for us to drive in his car and as I followed the sounds and directed him where to drive, we ended up about 20 blocks down towards

the Max Bell arena. It didn't take long to realize these explosions I heard were the sounds of the fireworks show from the Calgary Stampede. Yes, they were explosions but not the kind to ever worry about and it now made perfect sense why I didn't hear them impact the earth or a structure upon exploding.
Next of course, I had to acquaint myself with car doors being slammed shut, backfires, thunder and the occasional jet flying overhead. All of these to me sounded as though they roared through the universe and were almost deafening in sound, yet to all others around me, they could hardly hear any of it at all. It took quite some time to re-train my hearing to somewhat become normal again. A visit to the audiologist confirmed that I now had above average hearing and simply had to accept and teach myself that I was hearing more than anyone else could. Simple, I thought. But not so simple. Time would be the only way I would succeed at hearing what others heard and being fully aware of where I was, at any given time, would help me as well.

Meanwhile, life had a way of putting me in my place almost everywhere I went. All my hopes were eventually unrealistic dreams that I would finally begin to forget or bury down deep inside. One Sunday morning, I had gone to church and an older Croatian man I grew up with and knew quite well eagerly approached me and beamed a grin so wide I was truly surprised at his joy. He was normally such a stern, quite grumpy man, rarely smiled and always preached to us younger kids of how we were to live and how we should be behaving. This day, he seemed to think I was someone else, I thought, as I had never before seen him so genuinely happy to see me, or anyone for that matter.

"Tell me! Who has the popular vote back in Croatia?" He spat out his words so quickly as though he had been waiting for months to ask them of me. As I was completely caught off guard by not only his approach, his facial enthusiasm and his questioning political preferences, I stood staring back at him almost dumb founded. "Well!?" The color in his cheeks grew red and his eyebrows now began to touch, this was the man I recognized after all. His impatience was showing, and he shook his head, *"what's the matter with you?"*

I finally managed to say, "If you'd like to hear that all the money and clothing you and I helped raise last year never actually made it to the soldiers, or if you'd like to ask how the wounded are and if they have any messages for the outside world, *or even* if you wouldn't mind hearing of the ways in which people have survived such trauma and still find a reason to smile, this would be a far better topic to discuss than some political crap you have nothing to do with while living here in Calgary." And with this, the rumors began of how I went crazy overseas.

Even though I waited to see if I could remain calm and cool before speaking, I couldn't help or stop my response. I answered him with a response I could accept and truly believed he would accept it too. I spoke my truth. Once my reply was heard, his face looked as though it had lost every muscle within seconds then regained each muscle just as quickly as his color increased to a crimson, then an almost a blood red. He turned and stormed off as I stood there in the foyer of the Church waiting for the hymn to end. I stood and breathed, hushed myself and breathed again. I hadn't felt such anger in quite some time and worried of what I might say or do next. I felt my own face heat and was positive it may have been crimson as well.

Before leaving Church that day, I had several other men, the fathers, approach and ask me the exact same question of political preferences of the people I met in Croatia. Which political party was it that the civilians of Croatia rooted for. I was stunned and angry. I refused to answer these questions and in turn, my Dad of course heard from several Church members that perhaps his daughter needed some counselling as she was obviously not in the right frame of mind nor could she have a simple conversation. My Dad giggled when we discussed this on our way home but did advise that if I planned to return to Church, maybe I would entertain the possibility of humoring those with some political opinions. Of course, I refused to do this and instead, became quiet and seldom went to Church. I began being the outcast from our community and judgment gained ground. I soon realized what Milan must have felt like and giggled. Never would I have imagined being in a similar position to him with those I once knew so well, believing I had lost my mind. Yet here I was. I took Milan's approach and became quiet. The less I spoke, the more others would simply wonder yet have no real information to share in hopes to prove my odd behaviors, or, that I was actually crazy.

I had given up on sharing the truth within months following my return to Calgary. Friends, coworkers and people in general didn't want to hear the stories I so eagerly wanted to share. Either they were too horrified at the thought of them, full of disbelief or, any number of reasons I may never know. They simply didn't welcome my wish to share stories. As I became quiet and gradually played a role in the society I now belonged to, once again, I also slowly reintegrated myself into the society which I wanted to stay away from. With each day that passed I grew more a part of what was once so awful to me. I sat and listened to the everyday challenges my peers had, from where to go out for the weekend, to which studies they would be taking that semester at school. Time passed and I no longer had any ambition of changing anything, much less the world.

I was defeated and would simply become what was meant to be, a member of this world we lived in doing the mundane and daily chores of working and sleeping. Work and sleep. I joined the race I so hated and wasn't satisfied with just one job, I had three. My entire days were spent working and oftentimes I didn't have even a weekend to spare. I worked. I slept. Those around me were satisfied that I accepted becoming an adult, accepted responsibility and were impressed with my work ethic. I had peace. No one tried preaching to me any longer on how to become responsible or which paths to take. No one spoke of me, implying I would never amount to anything, that I was in need of counselling, or even that I wasn't working to my full potential.

I even dated for a bit, only to realize that this too was not really meant for me. The one relationship I thought just might work out, of course didn't. My crush for years, brightest blue eyes anyone had ever seen. His name was Alen. A few years of back and forth, always knowing we liked each other but never really doing anything about it. Finally, during my time back in Calgary, we dated but only for a short time. Within only a couple of months, he had threatened suicide at least once a week and I spent many nights trying to find him, or his supposed lifeless body, only to realize he was busy socializing with a new group of girls at yet another party. Many in our community, including my close friends, felt Alen and I were soul mates and destined to be together. Even I thought it for a time. The whispers were always present, almost like chants, that we were destined to be together. Of course, with my reintegration into regular life, I returned to the Church and my connection with Alen only helped gain me more respect. It was somewhat like a fantasy for everyone to share. What they didn't know was that it had been one of the most toxic relationships I would ever experience. Although he claimed he had loved me since he was as young as four years old, it felt far more like an obsession than love.

Alen would tell me how I was his reason for living. His every dream included me within them. His fate was to be with me and he knew it from such a young age. Then, after each profession of adoration or love, each beautiful compliment or show of affection, he screamed at me for just about anything imaginable and blamed me for all his miseries. I refused to own the obligation of being the sole purpose for anyone to keep living and, even though I felt strongly for him and we did have an undeniable connection, I made the choice to stop seeing him and would never look back. Even the times we went out together seemingly getting along were spent in arguments at the end of each night, him accusing me of making eye contact with some guy I never even realized was looking my way, or him accusing me of not really caring for him and simply pretending to want to be with him. He had endless reasons for blaming me for what he felt was a plot against him. He was a target and I apparently had such great aim, as did the rest of the world always out to get him.

After countless arguments and suicide threats, I finally ended our relationship one night before leaving him at a bar in downtown Calgary. When I got home, I found him parked outside my house late that very night, one wrist completely blood soaked. The blood was fresh and dripping onto his lap. He sat calmly, almost proud to have cut multiple slits into his inner wrist moving up towards his elbow several inches. I sat with him in his car and heard, yet again, how I was his only reason for living and that this time, with the blood-soaked arm as proof, he was ready to end his life. He claimed he would do the same to his other wrist should I truly leave him and end our relationship.

I looked in his beautiful blue eyes and knew I would miss them. As awful as it was, I would miss him and loved him. Then I asked him to please not end his life in front of my house and to have some respect by at the very least, driving down the block to end his life. As difficult as it was, I was no longer going to be the only reason for him to live, especially since he made it so impossible to make him happy. I knew that regardless if I stayed away from guys, or if I didn't question his flirtatious behavior, or any number of rules he had instilled into our relationship, he was ready to die at any time and made sure I knew it was always somehow my fault. I felt I had no choice but to say I could no longer be his reason to live and if I was, I wasn't able to help him any longer and simply wouldn't be that reason. I left his car, he drove off, and we both went on living separate lives.

The next step towards trying to build onto this responsible, adult life I was living was to go back to school and fulfil the last obligation I felt I had to society. Join the debt-ridden youth, then seek my high paying career path. I only lasted one semester at Mount Royal College in Calgary and although I completely enjoyed this type of education, I fought myself daily with my need for freedom. I wanted to complete a degree in Psychology but I also wanted to be free. My plan to complete two years at Mount Royal then transfer to the U of C would eventually only be a dream. Had I known I never would have returned to complete my degree, I believe I would have stayed and sought freedom afterward. Had I been able to think ahead and see my future, I would have fought myself to delay the temporary freedoms in order to gain a lifetime of success. Had I at least thought about it longer, I may have changed the course of my life.

Instead, I decided to travel to Croatia again after my semester ended and planned to return to school some day in the future when I was just a bit older. Psychology was definitely my goal, the timing simply wasn't quite right. I travelled to Croatia for another five month stay in 1994, then again for ten months in 1996. Constantly scribbling in my journals and hoping to one day share my stories. Constantly searching for somewhere to belong without all my doubts. Constantly believing that the inevitable would happen and I would become the adult I so disliked and pitied in my youth. It was simply meant to be and fate existed after all. Had I understood fate wasn't my enemy, rather a creation of the conditioning those who raised us instilled somewhere deep within, I would have understood it was all within my control. Some were strong enough to find their own way through and reach a life of happiness. Some were too consumed with doom, as I had been over time, and simply followed the pre-chosen path, ignoring the inner screams and warnings.

9 PART NINE
CHRISTMAS EVE 1997 TO MAY 15, 1999
CALGARY, CANADA
HAD I KNOWN, I WOULD HAVE RUN AWAY

I took the advice of my cousin Kerry and made the phone call. *What did I have to lose? Was I in love with him after all? Would I regret never making the call to find out if I actually made a mistake by leaving Croatia, yet again, while knowing I didn't want a future in Calgary? What was it that drove me away in the end?* I thought it was because I wanted more from life than spontaneity and it was time to really grow up. Sitting in my room catching up with my cousin who just returned from living in the States, I listened to myself as I spoke words of how much I loved someone yet ran away because it wasn't what this society I so rejected dictated to me after all. I left the life I wanted for a life I felt I needed.

What tore me between two worlds so much? Responsibility. *But who's idea of how life was supposed to be was more important?* Not mine. It was time I stood up for what I felt was right for me, regardless of what anyone else would think. Let them judge me. I finally realized I didn't care any longer for the judgments of others and that no matter what I would ever choose to do, someone, somewhere, would judge. It was time to free myself from the worry of those around me. I wasn't going to grow up and become this stable, responsible, day to day predictable person. Ever. I actually hated it. It made me miserable. That didn't mean I was unable to care for myself or provide for myself. It just meant I didn't need to one day own a yacht! *What was I thinking?* This was a huge relief! Kerry helped me in a way she may never truly understand and this was the best I ever felt about myself and my future. I was grateful and excited to feel such hope!

To get married, be stable and grow up. I never wanted to commit myself to marriage and although I wanted and dreamed of at least four children, I never imagined myself married. There was nothing wrong with this. Freedom! I wanted to sing and dance and celebrate my newly found freedom to go forward and live the only way I knew how. I was about to finally move forward without any solid plans, other than a promise to myself to live free and dream big. Whatever life would bring I would smile and enjoy the fact that I was living it. I dreamt of being a Mom since I was little, my entire life I felt this would be a career so to speak. Being a Mom. The biggest, most important job I could ever have. I would sacrifice all else to be a Mom one day. Nothing would be as important to me. I understood that everything would fall into place and be perfectly alright. I would follow my own path and this path was not set in Calgary.
I left Croatia late 1996 and a guy that was actually the perfect guy for me. He never dreamt of marriage nor did he have a thought of needing to plan an entire future in order to live. He lived day by day as I had. He wanted children just as I had. He never asked me to change and in fact, insisted that I didn't. He was happy with his life and I had finally been happy with mine. Then, as history had proven to me repeatedly, I allowed that little voice inside my head to win, making me run back to Calgary to try and become someone I wasn't. Someone responsible yet never knowing what this truly meant. Someone who needed to be something, anything except whatever it

was I was being. Always that little burden of guilt I carried whenever I was feeling content on my own, making my own decisions. Always some reminder of how I wasn't living according to plan, never understanding who's plan it was that I was to live by.

Kerry couldn't have come back at a better time and I thanked her for it. I had such clarity. Christmas Eve I made the call. I confidently dialed the overseas number and asked for him by name. His Military unit knew my voice well and although it had been at least a year since I last called, the man who answered chuckled when I asked for Mat and he instructed me to hold the line and not hang up. I laughed as he repeated himself and made me promise not to hang up, again. I assured him I wouldn't and then he ran to find him.

Within minutes Mat was on the phone, excited to hear from me. He was always happy and accepted me for who I was, regardless of how long it had been since we last spoke. He wasn't angry with me for leaving the country without a single word to him. He wasn't questioning my choices. He simply asked if he would see me again and when I planned to return. He was happy I called, not angry it took me a year to make the call. He didn't judge me but accepted that I was torn between right and wrong, torn between two lives and reassured me that regardless of what I would decide, he would always answer my calls.

Not knowing what to do as my regret was stronger than it had ever been, I asked if he would come to Canada to see what my life here was really like. I explained that if he could see this side of me and my life, then maybe I could figure out a way to make it all work and I would be able to finally close the Canadian chapter and move on. He agreed and explained that he would come and spend time with me and looked forward to seeing this other life I had. He said he would never live in Canada, as far as he believed at the time, but had nothing against being a part of my life here, so that my life in Croatia could finally begin. He agreed that it would be a great experience and knowing this other part of who I was could benefit us both. We both had something to look forward to. We were excited to begin this new chapter and I felt that I might finally find the answers I had always been searching for. I had so much hope that I nearly cried with relief. Relieved with this new outlook on life and so excited to soon begin plans for his travels. I readied myself for Midnight Mass at the Church I grew up in and the community that was like family, and hoped the night would end quickly so my plans could begin to come alive.

A long-standing tradition and although I almost stayed home, I attended the Midnight Mass at Church with so many others I grew up with. I was happy this night and made my rounds to wish everyone a Merry Christmas. As I was almost ready to go home, there he was, outside the Church doors surrounded by many we both knew. He stood with his arms open inviting me in for a hug. It was Alen. Several years had passed since the night I left him, bloodied in his car, ending a very bad relationship and moving forward with hope. There really was no reason to walk into his hug. His eyes so blue they practically glowed from a distance. We had a connection, even after the years that passed and the harsh words we spoke, the past suddenly disappeared and there he was, standing with his arms outstretched and those around us silently waited for my response. The whispers began.

I was too happy to be mad or dwell on the past. I was about to really begin living my life and thought maybe this was yet another way for me to make amends and move on. I suddenly let go of all those months I was driving him to either hospitals to wake him from a coma due to a drug overdose or searching for his lifeless body. I forgave his jealous rages and threats of suicide. I forgave him for all of the accusations he threw at me to inflict guilt and make me the owner of his miseries. There he stood, open armed with a smile so inviting I simply couldn't resist. *What harm could come of it*, I thought. He seemed so genuine. I walked into his hug and our friends began to whisper and laugh saying, him and I were meant to be after all. The small crowd was happy.

I was simply so relieved that my life was coming together that I didn't see any harm in walking into a hug. It was just a hug. A hug that did change the course of my life, regardless of what I believed at the time. A hug that ensured I never spoke with Mat again. A hug that would never be undone. Had I known what this hug had the power to do, had I known the path this would soon take me on, *I would have run away instead of slowly walked right into it*. I should have screamed and kicked instead of quietly succumb to the innocence he portrayed. I should have believed in myself and I should have called Mat to tell him of my confusion. Instead, I decided to see where this road would take me, believing that in the end, I would be back in Croatia in no time living the life I had always dreamed of, with someone who was as free spirited as I had always really been. I felt that I would start the plans for Mat's arrival within a couple weeks which wouldn't make much of a difference, and Mat would understand.

Within a couple of short months, Alen and I were seeing each other regularly. To say I was shocked at his transformation would be a total understatement. He was no longer insecure and spoke of life in such a new, inspirational way I had never heard from him before. He listened intently to all of my stories and was so proud of me, always encouraging me to share more and listening intently to each word I would speak. He caressed my hair, held me gently, whispered his love to me yet never made me feel trapped or unsafe. He created a beautiful, supportive life with me and as the months passed, he proved to me over and again that we were soul mates after all.

He openly discussed the past and asked for forgiveness for all the hurtful words he once spoke, horrible situations he had put me in and the multitude of times he threatened to end his life. He thanked me for leaving him as I did and said it changed his life. He took me on spontaneous road trips which overwhelmed me with joy. He welcomed my friends and we went on yet another road trip to visit my childhood friend, Rachel, who moved to Vancouver. We all spent a weekend together, even driving to Seattle for coffee, just because we could.

We drove up to the Yukon to visit my oldest sister Marija, and although the trip itself was a bit difficult, I was overwhelmed with the fact that he wanted to take it with me and actually made it happen. Everyone was happy we were together and even when we seemed to struggle, we were always reassured that the struggles were a normal part of all relationships. Everything seemed too good to be true and as the months passed, I still hadn't called Mat and soon felt that this was now to be left in the past and I was beginning my new life. This new life promised a future that would still allow me my freedom, yet Alen was happy to join me on any new adventure and experience without question. He seemed genuinely excited to live life the way I had lived life. We would build a future together with no regrets.

He spoke of a future that would never trap me and helped me see a future with many children was in fact possible, even in the City I had always tried to escape. He reassured me that regardless of my choices, whether to remain in Calgary or move across the seas, he would always love me no matter where I chose to be. He became my best friend and I believed I had begun to fall in love with him, and he was in love with me. Alen said that if I wanted him to, he would live anywhere in the world with me. Alen now was the one to steal my heart. I never believed in true love, but I knew it happened once before, and now, it happened once more.

In just less than a year of dating, Alen and I were engaged to be married. How it happened was quite simple. He became everything I never imagined existed in a man and I in turn agreed to marry him. His proposal was written in a card, placed in the drawer of his nightstand along with an engagement ring. I accepted this proposal and understood it was the only thing Alen ever really asked of me. This was his only request ever, to be married. He was open to a fun filled spontaneous life with me and said he would never ask me to change a thing about myself. He though, had a dream of marriage. I felt this was a compromise I could definitely accept and so we planned his dream wedding, not mine. The tough part came when I realized planning his dream wedding was actually, in fact, his parents' dream wedding and not his. The engagement was very short, only 5 months. Alen's parents had become a challenge, to say the least, and although I called the wedding off several times in just a matter of weeks following our engagement, the wedding remained scheduled for May 15, 1999 and I managed to get through the months prior to it without running away.

Alen promised with his heart and soul that once we were married and moved out into our own home, somewhere in this world, his parents would no longer be a part of our lives and he too would then have freedom. Together, we would live out our lives as I never imagined possible, free to live life day to day without the burden of society dictating to us who we should be and how we should live. *It would be worth it*, I thought.

Our wedding approached and plans had been made with very little input on my part. Alen's parents, Kreso, most Canadians knew him by Chris, and Mara were old school, traditional, from Bosna i Hercegovina themselves and felt they deserved to have a wonderful party to celebrate the wedding day of their first born. Kreso at the time was an influential businessman and made well over $25k each month. This was his 'on the books' income that is, as his off the books income most likely doubled that amount. They were always well dressed, jewels and all, classy and well spoken. Their presence was always noticed and they seemed to have the respect of many people, both within our community and in the business world. Mostly, they thrived when those around them were envious of them. This brought a certain sparkle to their eyes that almost had me believe they had souls somewhere within them. *Almost*. They had a history of throwing extravagant parties *just because* and were always ready to entertain. They were total opposites from my own parents who were literally down to earth and lived off the earth as well. My parents, known for growing their own garden while Alen's parents, practically owned the market and had others do the gardening for them.

Alen was different. He disliked his parents' lifestyle and always appreciated mine. He strived to be down to earth and disliked the fancy get-togethers and could hardly wait to leave them. Our wedding then, in my mind, was a small sacrifice for the freedom to come. As much as I now believed he would add to my life, I felt I would add to his. Even though, for the most part, I believed this would all end very well, I lost an incredible amount of weight due to the stress. My wedding dress and even bustier had to be specially tailored weeks before our wedding as I was smaller than a zero. I was thinner than I had been since I was a child. But, the show must go on as Mara reminded me when I begged for her to step back for a bit and give me some breathing room. She simply ignored my stress and played it off as normal bridal nerves.

My stress increased when the Priest decided that I should attend mass each and every Sunday and follow each of his rules or the wedding would be cancelled and everyone would of course, blame me for the cancellation. He even called me at home one Sunday when I missed the service and yelled at me. Alen on the other hand, never had to attend church and no one seemed to think twice about it. Yet again, Alen would remind me of the future and our freedom within reach. *Just hang on! We're almost there!*

With over 700 people attending the wedding and with my wedding gown fit for a princess and a train close to ten feet long, I quickly changed into my blue converse running shoes before the first dance began which irritated Mara to an extreme. She smiled as she quickly approached me from across the hall and while outwardly, she appeared to simply hug me, she fiercely whispered in my ear to change back into my satin pumps *at once*! I ignored her demand and continued on with my sneakers as the night moved along.

Originally, Mara had allowed Alen and I to choose our own song for our first dance and we agreed that the remainder would be her choice, as per her wishes. Eager to dance with my new husband to 'Iris' by the GooGoo Dolls and ignore my new Mother in Law, we waited for the music to begin, nervous with all the attention centered on us. I heard the click of the speakers and as the entire hall was silent, waiting for our first dance as husband and wife, the song began and instantly I realized I didn't recognize the song. It wasn't 'Iris'. It wasn't even a song I knew. It was a song, in Croatian that had no meaning to me at all. It meant nothing to Alen either. He could feel me tense and hushed me quietly while remaining calm. He continued to smile as did I. *Don't let everyone see, don't let everyone know.* He simply wanted to get through this night without having to worry and I was to help make this one and only dream come true.
It took more energy than I thought I had in me not to run and escape the night. I searched the hall for her and met her eyes, her dark yet shiny eyes and huge, fake smile as she watched us dance to her song. She truly enjoyed this and was showing the entire room a facade of pride and joy at her son dancing with his bride, yet all along, she was simply enjoying all the night's accomplishments she worked for months to create. Her wedding, her song,

her dress. Meanwhile Kreso, her ever loving husband, so proud his wife succeeded to pull it all off. The biggest party yet. As they both watched me closely, only I knew what their true thoughts were. They had no joy in their son's happiness, they only had joy from the 700 guests who showered them with compliments through the day and into the night. They never once asked what our wishes were for the wedding and went so far as to insist that the only wedding Alen and I would have, would one day come from our own children. That's simply how it worked. My only job on this day and night was to allow them this joy, this accomplishment. Moving forward, Alen assured me that they would have nothing, ever again, to do with our lives. Even Kreso and Mara had assured me of this many times and accepted that this wedding day would be their final farewell to any input they had in their son's life.

By the end of this wedding night we heard from so many of how Alen and I were destined to be together and that we made an incredible couple. They were so happy for us and were honored to be there in celebration with us. I succeeded in my promise to ensure no one knew of the immense stress and control placed on us by Alen's parents. I succeeded even though it was totally against my nature to convince even my own family that I truly was ok with it all. All I knew was that it was worth it as Alen wanted to live the life I had dreamed of with me, and all I had to do was get through a wedding in exchange. So simple I thought once, yet more difficult than I had ever imagined. I was relieved the night was over and I was left completely exhausted, both physically and definitely emotionally.

Both Alen and I made it through from engagement to wedding day and were finally free. He told me we would need to attend a gift opening back at the hall the following day, but this would then be the very last of our obligations. *One more day. Again.* Soon we would build our new life together and fulfill our dreams. Soon we would become what we often spoke of during our beautiful talks while sitting on hillsides from dusk until dawn. Soon, everything would finally come together and all of this would be a distant memory and we would be somewhere in the world, alone, creating a magical and happy life. He promised this to me as I promised it to him.

My new life was finally about to begin and I had someone to join me on the beautiful journey.

10 PART TEN
1999 CALGARY, CANADA
THE MIRROR SAW MY PAIN

It was really here. The day of a new life and freedom. The day that brought with it a sense of relief, peace and true joy. Alen and I woke in our Hotel room and I felt a calm peace which I hadn't felt in at least the past half year. Looking forward to this new, wonderful freedom, I brushed my teeth and looked to Alen excited to see what we would decide to do this first day of a new life. Alen was quiet. I thought he must be just as exhausted as I had been, but he simply needed to really believe we made it past the wedding and the gift opening the following day. Two days had passed since the wedding, *this was now the day that was our beginning!*

I suggested we go fishing! One of our wedding gifts from my brother and his girlfriend were two fishing rods with two awesome matching fishing hats! *What a great idea*, I thought. *How fun this will be*, I thought. I placed the funny green, large and loosely brimmed hat on my head and giggled showing Alen that this was a fun way to spend time and we should simply go find a lake and enjoy the day. He smiled wide and looked to be in full agreement and even placed his own hat on his head and smiled again. Then, as quickly as he had beamed his smile and seemed to love the idea, he shrugged. He shook his head and even said it was a great idea, but. That's all he said as he ended each idea I had come up with saying yes, sounds great, but. Finally, after several failed attempts at trying to tempt Alen out of the hotel room and into the open world outside, he said what was on his mind all along and distracting him from the joys of the world I had already begun to live, on my own, within my thoughts.

A few hours had already passed this wonderful day with the sun shining just outside the window to our room. Hours had gone by from the time I woke, full of zest and a will to get out and do something to celebrate, to the time I finally took my fishing hat off, sat on the bed beside Alen and was quiet. I waited. I now sat wondering if I had maybe forgotten something we might have planned? *Did I maybe forget that we had dreamt of this day already and thought of something else to do, and I may have disappointed him by forgetting?* I didn't think this could be as we had dreamt of the day, this day, when we had no plans and could simply get up and go do anything, without the need to plan. I was confused and felt a sudden burn in the pit of my stomach. *My stomach was trying to tell me something*, I thought. Maybe I was hungry.

Finally, Alen broke through my thoughts and I was thankful to hear his voice.

"Lou," he said with that beautiful, soft voice I loved. His eyes, although beautifully bright, looked sad. There it was, a moment where he was beginning to snap me out of the chaos in my mind by gently saying my childhood name, not nickname, but name. Everyone I grew up in our community who knew me well, knew I responded to Lou. Those who called me Lucy simply either didn't know me well or were angry. That's the feeling it brought naturally. Lou. My own parents called me Lou, my siblings, my friends, anyone close to me called me Lou. Funny how I would one day come to realize that when I mentioned childhood friends or those who knew me well, I only thought of the community I grew up in and not the friends I had in school, met through work or anywhere other than the community, the Church. There was our community, then there were the Canadians. Very simple.

I was coming back to myself and the chaos was just now beginning to clear up within me. I was already feeling some of the pressure that had so quickly built up begin to release. I eagerly awaited his words and for him tell me what wonderful idea he had. I decided that I would go along with and agree with whatever idea it may be! *Maybe he was only sad because he didn't think I would want to go where his thoughts had taken him? Maybe to the mountains instead of a lake close by? Maybe we would simply stroll through the neighborhood we stayed in?*

Or maybe he had planned a road trip as he used to do those days before our engagement took over our lives.

But why would he look at me like this? My smile went away, it left me. I tried to bring it back, but it simply didn't want to return. Once my smile was gone and there was no sign of its return, a slight curve formed at his lips almost reassuring me all would be ok. I understood, somehow, without any instructions required, that simply sitting here, no smile living within me and with no thoughts of what would happen next, Alen would finally begin to talk. *Finally*! I realized that it was my silence that was needed now. It was my silence that would allow for the day to move forward. How simple. I was somewhat relieved to have found this trick yet somewhat hurt that this was the trick. I was confused but calm. I surprised even myself at how I had gone from excitement and my heart racing with anticipation of the day, to a calm, quiet, almost sleepy state. This all happened when he simply sat still, yet finally made eye contact with me after what seemed hours of my babbling on about outings and excursions and, well, all my thoughts as he stared off to a blank wall of our hotel room. Now, I thought, we finally had communication. We had eye contact. I didn't feel alone in the room anymore and he was actually with me, not just in presence. This was great, I thought. So why did I feel so sad? My stomach again shot a burn but I ignored it, knowing we would soon be heading out and I would simply grab a bite to eat. Then, the burn would go away. I didn't want to lose this contact, this communication we finally reached so I sat still, kept my smile hidden within and was quiet. He finally spoke.

"We have to go through each gift card," he began quietly, still looking at me, still communicating. A numbness came over me and I was thankful to be seated on the bed and not standing. I was thankful as I suddenly couldn't feel my limbs and could only feel the pounding of my heart. It pulsed through my ears like a drumbeat, through my chest and in my wrists. I quickly looked down as I had many years ago during my first night in Ivankovo, when the bed I lied in trembled, and believed I would see my shirt move with every thunderous beat of my heart. I saw nothing. Without my permission and as I tried my best to hush myself and breathe, my eyebrows raised instantly then came together and my lips opened, yet I had no words. I looked back to Alen as he continued just now realizing he was still talking. "My parents need a list of every gift we received. There's a pad of paper in the box with the cards and if you wouldn't mind," he looked over to the box by the desk under the oversized mirror, "I will open the cards and tell you the amounts and you can write the list." He finally smiled.

There it was, the smile and the slight glisten in his eyes. Smiles always made life better and had a magical power to transform even the most awful situations, I thought. He finally smiled on this bright day for the first time. All morning I had been looking forward to his smile and here it was. Looking directly into my eyes, finally, smiling sweetly as my stomach burned even hotter and my heart pounded even louder and I felt the warmth in my eyes, as the first tear made its way down onto my cheek. I had no smile. This was now easy for me, to not smile. Looking directly at me, Alen seemed to see none of these events happening to me. He didn't see my sadness or my heart wanting to leap from my body. He didn't see the pain and burn in my stomach or even the tears now streaming and falling from my cheeks.

Maybe I was past exhaustion, I thought. Maybe I was dreaming. Maybe the stress had finally gotten to me and I would wake up, and Alen had never even become part of my life at all again. Maybe, *just maybe*, I could die. Maybe I could die and everything would go away. There would be nothing left for me to question. I wouldn't have to ever feel disappointment again. I wouldn't have to wonder why I spent so many years fearing the judgment of others, while never being able to name one single person I was judged by. I would no longer have to feel the burn in my stomach as I had felt over the past months since the engagement, and I wouldn't have to force myself to eat even though I knew I desperately needed to. I would no longer have to see Kreso or Mara or hear of the tasks we still, even after the wedding was now done, have to complete in order to move on. I had made my mistakes. I had run away and toward them many times already. I no longer wanted to run and had no more energy for it. I was tired. Just stop. I wished everything would simply, stop.

"*Lou!*" Alen shouted. I shook my head as though I was a cartoon figure resetting myself and gasped for air. Had I stopped breathing? It felt as though I was drowning and his shout brought me a sudden rush of air. I desperately tried to ignore all my thoughts and bring my focus back to him, to his face, searching for something to bring me back to safety. "This is all we still have to do!" he said desperately, "*then we are free!*"

I whispered and forced a small smile to my face and spoke, "Okay." Now it was me who seemed to be unable to look him in the eye. Now it was me who seemed to have no desire to go out and enjoy, anything. I wanted to hide, not explore. I wanted to sleep, not go fishing. Then within seconds, I didn't know what I wanted. It suddenly didn't matter what I wanted, even to myself. *Maybe I missed something*, I thought. Maybe he had told me at some point, through the past several months of absolute tension and anxiety, that we were to do this one final step before freedom finally finds us. I must have forgotten. That had to be it. This was, at least, something I could live with and helped me to not want to hide, to sleep, to shrink away, to die. For the first time in my life, I felt the will to die and this terrified me. I wiped my tears myself as he still hadn't even mentioned them, they didn't exist.

Although he stared right at me, he must not have seen my tears. *Maybe they weren't even real*, I thought. As I wiped my cheeks and eyes I realized that still, he gave no mention to them or acknowledged my pain. I didn't know what to think anymore. Stop thinking and just breathe. That's all I could do and that's all I did as I went and picked up the heavy box from by the desk, noticed myself in the mirror before turning to bring the box to the bed. The mirror saw my pain. It saw the redness of my eyes and the glisten from droplets I missed while wiping them away. It saw how hungry I had been and still was. It saw everything. I refused to look at the mirror many times moving forward in life. I would pass by them and look down. Moving forward, I would simply forget the day my avoidance and dislike of mirrors had begun. This very day, while sitting beside my husband, writing names beside dollar amounts beside more names and even more dollar amounts, I kept my head down.

Alen was now full of joy and excitement explaining that once we were done with the cards, the list and the duty we had to fulfill for Kreso and Mara, yet again, we would go out and book our honeymoon travels. This brought me some comfort, some hope and a small ray of light began to shine again. The ray of light was far duller than ever before, but it was there. I could see it. It took until the following day to visit the travel agent as the amount of gift cards we received were so numerous, the process of creating the list for Kreso and Mara took us well past midnight.

The following day brought with it some excitement and the reward for following our instructions, our duty. Alen surprised me when we approached the travel agent and he asked for two tickets, seated next to each other, anywhere in the world leaving the following day. This is how our honeymoon to Saint Martin in the Caribbean came to be. A wonderful story that I would soon see brought so many people envy and brought Alen, so much joy. The story of it, not the journey. So many thought the story so romantic, they looked at Alen with new found respect, adding to an already existing wander they had with those beautiful eyes he had, the sweet smile, his gentle voice, the fast car, his great career and a guy he portrayed himself to be. The envy that made Kreso and Mara's eyes glisten and their lips smile so wide, everyone simply thought they were happy people enjoying their lives. I saw it now, I saw it too late.

Promises bring hope. They are those tiny rays of light at the end of dark tunnels that, when you ease your way closer to them, they grow and shine brighter and lead the way to the open road and freedom away from the dark, cold walls that enclose us. They are what bring the dawn after the dusk. Promises are words to lead us out of or even into darkness. Such weight, such power these words woven then spoken, creating promises. They bring with them the hope.

I promise.

11 PART ELEVEN
1999 CALGARY, CANADA
THE PROCESS OF ACCEPTANCE AND OWNING MY DECISIONS

My Mom picked us up from the airport and told us that she suffered third degree burns to her upper legs and abdomen. I felt awful for her yet knew she didn't look for sympathy. She was strong. Even with her burns, she picked us up smiling and was excited to ask how our honeymoon had been. While I explained the beauty of the island and how planes landed so close above the beach, the fact I was scared of a dolphin when Alen and I had gone on seadoos to a mini island exploring and how we lounged in the pool enjoying the beautiful sun, Alen remained quiet as though he was hearing of the stories for the first time and tried to imagine them. Finally, Alen spoke and shared that he had scratched his pinky toe in the ocean, and it was very painful but seemed to now be healing. Yes, I apologized to Alen as I neglected to mention his painful scratch and met his eyes that seemed to say, you don't care. I felt a sudden guilt and apologized for not relaying this, to Alen, most important part of our trip. Alen gave me a reassuring smile and chuckled that of course it wasn't something I would remember to share, it had only happened to *him*. I felt a shot of pain in my stomach. This wasn't why I forgot to mention it and as I began to defend myself, he quickly looked back to my Mom and asked how she was managing her burns. I listened as they spoke wondering if I was selfish after all but kept this to myself, as Alen then moved on to ask how everything else had gone while we were away.

My Mom continued to tell us of some very sad news that one of our childhood friends from our community had taken his life while we were away. Too many guys we knew through childhood and in our community ended their lives and Alen suddenly looked at me with eyebrows joining in anger. He blamed me. That's what I understood immediately. He blamed me, somehow he was angry with me. My Mom noticed and questioned him immediately. Alen bounced back into his beautiful, peaceful expression with eyebrows now innocent and accepting while he simply explained the sun was in his eyes. He apologized to her for giving the wrong impression and of course, he must be tired from the trip and the pain he had experienced in his foot. After all, he went on to explain, he suffered through the pain to ensure our trip was a success and to not ruin it for me. He was so selfless, so giving. I was about to add that his pain hadn't even begun until we were leaving Saint Martin but he quickly continued, so I remained silent and didn't interrupt. I'd explain it soon, once he was done, I thought. He continued, saying he was saddened by the news of our friend and wished he had been able to attend the funeral. He was now just tired and simply needed to rest. Small talk got us quickly to my parent's house and I simply felt awkward to bring up what I had wanted to earlier confirm, that he hadn't relayed a proper version of his story and made it sound as though he suffered the entire trip, but realized it would now seem completely out of place in the conversation. I let it go.

After my Mom had given us some privacy once we reached her house, I questioned Alen why he seemed angry earlier with me and told him I was now angry myself. I felt as though he somehow blamed me for the suicide and knew this was simply outrageous. I also added that I in no way didn't feel that his scratch wasn't important, but wanted to share our good stories with my Mom as for the most part, our trip was enjoyable and the scratch had only actually happened the very last day of our trip. He reassured me that he wouldn't be the reason for me to be sad or angry and would do his best to pretend to have joy.

With all he said, he did the very things he said he wouldn't do and I struggled to understand what I was feeling. I found myself more and more confused when questioning Alen on anything. I had been fighting the feelings of defeat and fatigue now for roughly 6 months. I still struggled with understanding and accepting my life choices the year before. I had once been so strong and so determined to moving forward and yet found myself now, whenever I began to put effort in to moving forward, feeling pushed back and defeated whenever he spoke. He was often silent and I soon grew to like it more this way, almost like a break from feeling run down. When he would talk, I'd only get confused or be left feeling tired, even guilty, and that awful burn in my gut would make its appearance.

We walked farther from the house to have some privacy and talk. I wanted to understand what was truly going on with Alen and explain how his reactions were quite upsetting to me. I soon wished I stayed in the house, close to my parents, as this walk seemed suddenly far away from anyone who helped me feel normal. Being alone with Alen since the wedding had become not just awkward, but somewhat scary. I didn't think I knew him and was overwhelmed to think I was married to him, committed to him. I made this promise in front of hundreds of people who truly believed we were soul mates and that we were happy. Hundreds of people who, as Alen had many times reminded me since, looked down on me and finally accepted me back into the community we grew up in. Finally, I was realizing that the best part of marrying Alen had been the absence of feeling judged. It felt freeing to realize I no longer had the constant feeling of being judged from afar, without understanding exactly how this ever came to be. The community that we shared since childhood and was such a constant, now looked with acceptance, approval and little to no judgment. Almost as though it really was meant to be. We were destined to be together, we were soul mates. Right after this awful, forced performance, the only positive that had come of the wedding, the marriage, I realized, was in fact I now had freedom from judgment.

Alen spoke and I was quietly listening. I was back in the moment, thinking and listening only to his words and not rejoicing in my new awareness of how free I was from the burden of judgement. We walked slowly, close together as he whispered all the negative emotions he said he felt and that he insisted, I made him feel. From a distance, had my parents been watching, they would see a couple in love, looking down while taking a nice, beautiful walk around the yard, sharing a beautiful day together. Up close, it was an attack on me and my mind, my soul, my already weakened state. It felt like our wedding night, when Mara rushed towards me, seeming to give me a hug yet demanding I change back into my pumps. What everyone thought was most important and this is how we would accomplish our goals. If we kept up the appearance, we would be freed.

Now, Alen was like Mara, seeming to be taking a leisurely stroll with me while ensuring I heard every accusation very clearly. Every insult. Every word he threw at me to bruise me, to make me fall. Now he spoke quietly, only to me, that the trip was a mistake while reassuring me that he wouldn't allow this to ruin my great feeling, my need to hold on to the positive or my wish for another trip to come.

He explained how he only wished for me to be happy and that my happiness now meant the world to him. He said he would accept that I didn't care for his happiness. He said he would find a way to ensure my happiness continued, regardless of his pain and sadness. My head started spinning and I felt weak, very weak. I interrupted several times only to be ignored. I grew angry, then more tired. *Had he really not enjoyed the trip at all?* I replayed some of the days and remembered he smiled, laughed, snorkeled. I questioned him, begging him to help me understand what he was actually saying as I couldn't understand it at all.

He sighed and whispered, "See Lou, that's just it right there. You really don't even have a clue how I feel or what I'm going through." I was now so angry with this! I stopped and began spitting words out, refusing to accept his accusation and insisted he now listened to me! He kept walking. He kept walking slowly, head down, shoulders hunched. To anyone watching, if they had been, it would look as though I had simply and quite suddenly, went mad, lost my cool for no reason. He was such a victim now. Head down, walking away as I was obviously angry with him, shouting after him, the poor guy. All he appeared to want was to make *me* happy and he was unable to accomplish this, as I was simply selfish and heartless. I wanted to scream but in no way wanted my parents to hear me, hear my anger or think anything was wrong. Afterall, it was now well after the wedding, things were to be great and this was why we all went through the immense stress of a wedding fit for kings, regardless of our simplicity.

I felt tired all over again and a weight began to push my shoulders down, my head lowered, and I quit. I simply quit. I hated to argue and saw that it only made me more tired, accomplishing nothing else. Alen knew this as he knew everything about me. He knew. *He knew!* He simply ignored me and walked on. He continued to walk away from me and remained sad, regretful and outright told me it was my fault. It was me who had brought this to him. I was so tired. Each day that went by the past few months, I spent more energy trying to feel alive only to become more tired with each attempt. I quickened my pace catching up to him, not wanting my parents to think anything was wrong, not knowing if they saw us or not. Another wonderful trick Alen had taught me before our wedding. He taught me to remember people were always watching, even when we didn't think they were. Easy enough for me to understand, Milan had once said the same thing to me and he was right. But Milan would never treat me like Alen did. Milan and I never hid because of a need to prove our worth or acceptance, we hid to avoid wasting time with silly questions and nonsense. Even though Milan and I had been great friends and nothing more, we hid to avoid rumors twisting the great friendship we had cherished. Now, if my parents had been watching, they would definitely say something and question why I was so upset and this of course wouldn't have helped anything. My parents would most definitely step in, they'd react. Who wouldn't? I couldn't let them see this.

I buried my anger and saved what little energy I now had. It was *my* decision to go through with the wedding even though I repeatedly called it off and even though my family tried to pull me out of it. It was *my* decision to put on the act, the show for our community to be able to enjoy the party. It was all on *me* to work through this. To find a solution. It was *me* who had put my family in a position to be happy for me at the wedding, to celebrate a new life and ignore any signs of stress as it was all so worth it, to *me*. It was *my* fault. I had been selfish after all! I was the one who ultimately played out a fairytale wedding I never wanted! I was the one who hid my true feelings and faked happiness in front of not just my family, but an entire community! I was the one who said it was all going to be worth it! For what? *For me.* Selfish. Yes. I realized I was selfish. Alen was right.

"Let's get our stuff together and head to my parent's house before supper. I need to clean up and get ready for work tomorrow." Alen said this with confidence once we were back at the house and he was already reaching for the front door. His tone was different, almost emotionless as he stated what we were now to do. This wasn't a question. It wasn't something we had previously discussed and it was in no way something I expected. I knew this now. I didn't even question myself or if I had maybe forgotten a plan. This was his decision and this was what we were now going to do. I was exhausted, weak and now, full of self-blame. I was selfish. I may have wanted to argue Alen on his accusations and I may have wanted to defend myself just moments ago, but now, I accepted I had been selfish and knew there would be no point in arguing. I had been selfish, not in the way Alen wanted to make me believe but that didn't even matter anymore. Being selfish was now a trait I had to own, myself, for my own reasons. So, this is what I accepted and this feeling of absolute weakness was my fault as well.

How I had become so selfish was something no one, absolutely no one could help me overcome as I made every decision on my own, as I always had. I always accepted responsibility for my choices, regardless of what they may have been. Alen opened the door, my parents smiling at our return, asking how our walk had been. I saw that they gave us our privacy after all while we were outside walking. They had no question in their expressions. They were simply happy we were there.

With his sweet voice and his eyes now transformed from piercing with accusation, to suddenly angelic and beautiful as he said his thank you's to my parents, he explained that him and I were heading to his parent's house as he would be returning to work. They seemed surprised but saw that we were together and all was ok. We were now a married couple and we had no reason to give them reasoning behind our decisions. I stood behind Alen, smiling to ensure no one expected anything other than joy. Smile. *Just smile.* Everyone was always reassured with a smile. I was done hurting anyone, any longer. No one else in my world would now have to accept responsibility to help me, to guide me, to warn me of any choices or paths I took. The community was content. My family, now content. Everyone believed Alen and I were happy, meant to be and this was what I created. This was what I allowed. This was what I asked for.

The freedom I believed would come following the wedding, it was

promised to me by three people and in turn, I promised it to everyone I knew. I refused to break my promise. I believed three people who I knew for a fact lied to the world around them. I believed I was different and that they would never be able to lie to me. I was selfish, and now quickly added stupid to my traits. How stupid I had been. I put on my smile and ignored the burn in my stomach and held back the tears. Easy now. It was totally my fault. Of course!
During our drive, my tears flowed like never before and once again I was alone in my pain. Alen drove, listened to his music and said nothing. I was glad to look down, avoiding even the tiny side view mirror and be alone with my thoughts. *Everything would be okay one day*, I thought. I finally realized that it would all be okay and I would be the only one who could make it okay. Yes, I knew I was exhausted. Conversations with myself had become my way to pass the time and hope that Alen wouldn't speak, wouldn't add to what I had already begun in my mind, the process of acceptance and of owning my decisions, my life.

Since the wedding, Alen whipped insults and reminded me of my flaws every now and then. I didn't want him to speak now, I wanted him to just drive. I didn't yearn for him to see my pain, I simply wanted to feel it, by myself. Just be silent, I begged within my own thoughts for him to just remain silent. He did.

I would go see a Doctor, I thought. I reassured myself that mistakes are okay unless we let them control us. I pretended to be a shrink, to myself, within my own thoughts. This even made me slightly giggle, just quiet enough that Alen didn't even hear it over his blaring music. I reassured myself, again within my thoughts, that I would soon see my Doctor and see if she would help me. She wasn't involved with this whole mess I created. I would go to her and ask for help. *No one would even have to know.*

Alen was so content driving with me beside him, on our way to live with two people we both swore we would stay away from. How silly I was to ever believe his words, their words, when all I witnessed was the opposite from each. How stupid I must have been to think they would follow through with their promises when I saw, all along, they spat lies to anyone who would listen and showed no regret, ever. How stupid I was to believe Alen's promises. He hadn't been the Alen I dated for almost a year immediately after I accepted his proposal, in a card, from his nightstand, with no other written words of what I was getting in exchange for marrying him. I accepted this proposal and simply believed in his words. Oh I wanted to laugh out loud at myself. How stupid I was, how stupid I am.

I finally stopped sobbing and reassured myself that I would find a way to move forward and to bring back my self-control. Only I could do this. I was the problem and I would be the only one who could fix it. I was the one who allowed myself to get really sick. I was the one who allowed myself to be tired, hungry, sad, hopeless, all the things I had never experienced on this level, ever before, and I was the one who was now responsible to fix this. I was sick and I would see a Doctor, very soon, and get help. So simple. There was that glitter of hope again. The tiny spot of light calling to me at the end of the tunnel I travelled in for so long now. I saw it and I would have to reach it before I slip into hopelessness once again. I drifted into a beautiful sleep and escaped from life.

Our first home in Beddington, Calgary.

12 PART TWELVE
1999-2000 CALGARY, CANADA
I WAS HAPPY ENOUGH

I could breathe again. I woke to find that although I knew I still didn't feel back to my old self, I was on the path to recovery! I had been on the antidepressant just under a month and I began to feel some relief. Yes! I was so grateful to be alive, finally! I made it through what the Doctor explained to be quite a serious depression mixed with malnutrition. The words anxiety, stress and fatigue were repeated through his diagnosis and I listened, for the most part.

The day I wanted to finally see my Doctor and had an opening where I could excuse a longer absence from home, she had no available appointments so I took myself to a walk in clinic instead. I was determined to get help and as difficult as I knew this would be, and to talk about my true feelings after hiding them for so long, I had to do this on this day. I may not get another chance!

That day, I was determined to be as honest as I could with this man, this Doctor. He had nothing to do with my community or my family and would be neutral. I explained everything I had felt for far too long to this Doctor who seemed to genuinely want to hear me out. It was difficult to tell him that I felt like dying and regretted the past year of life, but I did. I told him. No one else would know. This was confidential and I didn't have to worry about judgment, what a relief!

Then, it was even more difficult to tell him I missed my freedom and had already forgotten what it felt like. I knew I once had it but it was now gone. As much as I didn't want to say these things out loud, I said them! I had to take this seriously and ask for help. I knew I wasn't getting better on my own. I knew that the old me would never feel this awful and this wasn't something I wanted. I still remembered the old me, I missed her and simply couldn't figure out how to get back to living her life.

The Doctor was quite concerned and took me seriously. He offered to get me into a type of treatment, but I refused this. This frightened me as then everyone would know, everyone would find out that I failed them and broke my promise. I pleaded with him to give me three months and if after this I still wasn't better, then I would agree to get more help. I knew I still had a will to live somewhere inside, I simply needed some help to find it again and keep going. I needed to find the energy again to make my own choices and not feel as though I didn't trust myself to do so. I needed to be able to trust again. *I wanted it*. I believe he saw that I still had fight in me and agreed to a trial period and prescribed me antidepressants. He explained it might take some time for them to begin working and they might not even be the correct type for me. I listened and understood all that he said and left. It took everything I had not to ask for something different, something that would make me feel great, now. I wanted to feel better and part of me knew this would take time, part of me wanted the fix to be instant. I resisted the urge for a quick fix and focused on giving myself time.

Looking back to that day in Alen's car, I made a promise to myself while I cried as Alen drove us to his parent's home and I was ignored and silenced once again. I consoled myself within my thoughts. After I awoke from my beautiful sleep, my escape, I promised myself I would get help and would find a way to see my Doctor without anyone else knowing. It would be kept to myself. Too many times had I found only trouble when I told Alen, anything.

I would go see my Doctor within days I reassured myself. In the meantime, I would *accept whatever* came my way and not allow myself to give up. I would not quit. I thought of the many great people through the years who, although they would never know, gave me the strength now to make this promise to myself and follow through. Those who lived through such trauma, witnessing brutal killings of loved ones. Those rebuilding their homes immediately after they were hit by rockets. Those who shared their dreams with me not knowing if they would return from the battlefield, and those who fought for their freedom so long while praying to stay alive to simply, keep living. My own parents who battled discrimination and fought for their own freedoms, making a life in this Country where they didn't even speak the language or understand the culture.

I told myself that this, what I was going through, was not only something I myself had chosen, but it wasn't even close to their stories, their lives. My enemy was created with my consent. I walked into it. I would need to find a way to walk out of it. I would do this. I would do this on my own as it was my own creation. My own, stupid choices brought me here. So many others had it worse. I shook my head as more tears streamed.

What in the world was I crying about? Really, *I had nothing to cry about*, I told myself. I would find my way back to living. I had to find a way without hurting the hundreds of people I lied to, convincing them I was happy when I wasn't. I couldn't die because my family would never forgive themselves for not forcing me out of the situation and instead believing in my words. I knew this is how they would feel even though it was so far from the truth. They tried to save me so many times and I didn't listen. I believed it would all work out! I reminded myself I hadn't died in a war zone, what in the world had brought me to this feeling now in a country of absolute peace? *A simple wedding? A stupid marriage?* I couldn't allow my pain to create a lifetime of regret for so many others. I was only one person. This was on me. I would win this battle and find my self-control again. I would simply accept whatever came my way in the meantime. I had to. This was how I would survive my own demons fighting me, asking me to quit. Acceptance.

And so, I accepted our return to Alen's parents' home. I accepted they only wanted to talk about how much everyone loved their party and how people would talk about this wedding for many years to come, they had outdone themselves. I accepted that Alen went back to work and I was left alone with Mara and Kreso many times as Alen worked late and on weekends. I accepted that Alen had told me to cancel my acceptance to SAIT for the travel program I enrolled in as he would be too afraid that I would never return had I travelled in any way. I accepted that I went with Alen several days in a row to the hospital upon our return as the scratch on his foot had become infected with e coli, and I accepted he blamed me for his near-death experience. I accepted he said I was selfish and nearly killed him with my travelling dreams and he would never travel with me again.

I accepted that he continued to go out, with old friends and new ones, and partied without wanting to tell me where he would be much less inviting me to go along. I accepted that he made the decision with his parents that him and I would buy a house in Calgary. I accepted that soon after we moved into our first home in Beddington, he said we now had to be responsible adults and work toward paying off our mortgage. I accepted that shortly after we moved into this house, he left for Libya for work and didn't return for almost a month. I accepted that Mara called me daily while Alen was away and questioned me on everything I had done each day, and I accepted that I could not ignore these calls. When I had ignored them, Alen called me to ensure I understood that I upset his Mom and this was not helping him focus on the work he needed to complete in Libya, his safety was in jeopardy and I was making things much worse for everyone. I accepted that Alen still called his Mom even while working overseas and they discussed me.

I accepted that he convinced me to quit my job with the insurance company as he felt downtown was unsafe and he constantly had to worry about me. I accepted that once I quit as he wanted, he accused me of free loading and being uneducated and worthless. I accepted that he hated my old car so we sold it and went into even more debt, as he picked out a brand new car we would have to commit monthly payments to, in addition to our new mortgage. I even accepted when I told him I was going to return to Mount Royal and work on my Psychology degree, accepting responsibility and adulthood, he refused this and shouted at me that I would only be inviting 'psychos' into our lives and how unbelievably idiotic that would be for me to do. Thoughtless. Selfish. Stupid. Childish. Yes.

All of this I accepted as it was my promise to myself to *stay alive*. I accepted it all so *I would not want to die*. I did not want to go through the embarrassment and humiliation of anyone ever finding out what a coward I had become and what I allowed into my own life, on my own. *I did this*. I agreed to this arrangement in exchange for a life with Alen. The Alen pre-engagement, but it was Alen nonetheless. *I deserved this*. I followed through with the wedding even though I had backed out many times, I still went through with it in the end. *This was all on me*. This is what I believed. I had always been a truthful person but I lied to everyone just so I could have a life with Alen. I believed Kreso and Mara when they told me they would let him go, even though I watched them lie to others daily. *That was on me. Only me*. Now my only goal was to keep going, accept and find help. Alone. I couldn't even entertain the thought of adding humiliation, regret and cowardice to this list. No, I had to do this on my own. Oh the judgment that would return if I didn't do this on my own was too great. I refused to allow the only thing that kept me from true happiness so long ago, to return its ugly head and win.

Alen returned from Libya and life continued with my full acceptance. He seemed much happier with this new me. I was even complimented a few times which surprised me considerably. Once I realized my antidepressants had begun to work, with excitement and more confidence than I felt in a long time, I finally told Alen of my visit with the Doctor and how I started to feel the pills were beginning to work. It had been quite some time since I spoke to him openly. I admitted to him that it was only a tiny bit of change and it had only just begun. I admitted that I still cried uncontrollably but it wasn't daily now and although I still felt trapped, I was happier and felt I would soon be back to my old self and saw there was a light at the end of this tunnel!

Alen sat silent and listened. He was so quiet. I focused on him intently otherwise I would definitely believe I was alone. I physically saw him there and finished explaining my situation and what led me to this wonderful place where I felt I could trust him again and spoke the truth.

After I stopped talking, I sat and watched Alen, still quiet, still motionless. Then, in an instant, he leaped from the couch and his body seemed to grow twice its regular size as he stood in front of me. I gasped as I was so caught off guard, I couldn't quite understand what was happening and felt as though sirens were blaring, warning me to seek shelter, *take cover!* I didn't move. He appeared to be taller than ever before and all his muscles swelled with thick veins spreading over tight skin within seconds. His face was now dark red, two veins seemed to pulsate above his eyebrow and his eyes literally glowed as he now stood, directly in front of me, only inches between us, hovering as I still sat on the couch, now cowering.

"You have the *nerve* to tell me that *you're* depressed?!" He shouted. I never knew his soft voice had such strength and intensity. My ears hurt from how loud he shouted. My ears rang and the buzzing began. It was a reaction I normally had under control for years but this reaction still occurred if I was caught off guard, not expecting loud noises. My body would return to a survival state and only hear the loud sound over all others. My mind would immediately begin to try and determine where the threat was originating, and my heart would pound through my entire body as I struggled to process my surroundings. This though, my mind seemed to be unable to process as it was directly in front of me, inches away. The threat was different than ever before. The sound was deafening and my head now hid behind my hands as I cowered even lower trying to protect myself. Instinct told me to run and hide but I couldn't. Alen blocked my exit with his power and stood so I was unable to flee. Instinct told me to seek shelter, but again, I couldn't move so my hands covered my head, by back hunched as low as it could go and I sought shelter in place. Nothing to protect me from shrapnel, from the fierceness in his voice and his vibration radiating and hitting me like nails.

"*You?!* You are the one that made me change into someone I'm not! You are the one who was nothing without me! You are the one my parents are embarrassed of and we all accepted you regardless of what the entire community thought about you! You are crazy! They all knew it for years and now that we took you in they finally accept you! You should be grateful *to us!*" He was gasping for air as his words almost ran each other over while he spat them out. I could feel the vibration of him still standing before me, hovering and shouting down at me as my eyes were closed tightly and my ears literally rang with pain. "Without us you would have nothing! Without us you would be nothing!"

I closed my eyes and covered my face now, letting my ears go. I held my eyes closed with my trembling hands and finally, with the little energy I had left, I fought to regain myself. I fought my mind and screamed at myself to regain strength and fight! I brought myself into the now and made myself aware I wasn't on a battlefield, *I was in my own home!* I tensed my leg muscles and felt the heat burn through them. I straightened my back and convinced myself that I was taller than Alen had ever been. I lowered my hands and tensed them, spread each finger, now pumping with energy, onto each side of me as I used whatever force they had and shot myself up from the couch and stood, not even an inch separating me from this monster that hovered over me. I lifted my head and met his eyes and shouted back. I shouted and I was certain I had veins of my own pumping fiercely now, albeit much smaller than his, but they were there and he could see them! I shouted up toward him, as he stood directly in front of me still, towering above me, I stood my ground and shot back at him!

"*We are done!*" I shouted. "You can have this house or move back with your parents, but we are done! You are done! You are done torturing me and making me pay for the biggest mistake of my life!" My throat sore as I had never in my life shouted as I had just then. I walked away confidently, each muscle still burning providing me the power to move, to leave, to walk away. I was done! This was now finally over! I went to the bedroom and grabbed only a few things, I genuinely didn't need much, and was at the stairs to leave within minutes. He stood, blocking my way. I was so angry I demanded he move! There was no way I could physically move him so I demanded again, that he move out of my way! I was ready for a fight and would not back down!

His muscles weakened, they lost their fullness almost as quickly as they came, they left. His veins began to disappear as though they never surfaced, pulsating with anger, they were now gone with no trace left. His eyebrows lowered as his eyes released a flood of tears and he stood, cowering before me. Now it was Alen with his head lowered, back hunched and hands trembling. He moved. With his back now bent, posture completely gone away, he slowly moved away from the stairs where he blocked my exit, my escape. His whole being was defeated as he cried and went to take his seat on the couch where this had all began. I stood at the stairs staring at his every move. As my heart still raced, my body began to weaken more than it had ever before. It was now past exhaustion for certain. I had used whatever little energy I had left over the months. I used it all now and I felt I could barely keep myself standing. I fell to my knees and sat on the floor, so weak. I watched as his face, drenched with tears I had never witnessed before, was now full of anguish, not anger. My heart sank. My stomach shot the burn I was all too familiar with and as I conditioned myself to ignore it for so long, I ignored it once more.

"You don't get it, do you," he quietly spoke. "It kills me when you cry. It kills me when you're unhappy. You don't get it." He continued to speak while I sat at the stairs, still believing I would leave once I had the energy to get myself up again. *I should have left.* I should have done as he had done so many times before and ignored his tears. I should have left and allowed him the time to look into the mirror. Instead, I sat and listened as he explained that I was the only one in his life who loved him.

His own parents lied to him his entire life and had never loved him. They always made promises they never intended to keep. I kept my promises. He learned from me. He wanted to see me happy and it was killing him that I wasn't, and this was why he was so lost, so cold, so angry. He said that when I told him of my depression, he felt as though he failed me. He said everyone would know he failed as a husband and that his parents were right all along when they told him that he would never succeed without them. He said so much. He said he was sorry. He said he just needed some more time to break the bond that his parents created and raised him with to keep him close. He desperately wanted to be free of them but had no idea how to do this.

"Don't you understand, Lou? I've been tortured my whole life and you're the only one who can help me. The only one who understands and sees my parents for who they really are, but you're still with me. Well," he paused, "I guess that's over now."

I managed to move myself to the couch. I sat, hugged him and he cried uncontrollably. I was quiet. I knew he was right when he said I did see his parents for who they really were. I hated them for how they treated me. I hated them for how they treated Alen. I hated how they treated everybody. I knew he was now telling the truth. I knew he had it in him to be a kind, compassionate person who at one point truly cared for me. Now, I was his only hope.

He finally spoke again, "Those antidepressants aren't what you need Lou. They'll just poison you. I'm sorry I haven't been very honest with you but I was too afraid to lose you. I'll do better, I promise. Please stop taking them because you wouldn't even need them if I had just been honest with you."

And with that, life took yet another new path and yes, I stopped the pills. The poison. Alen had been as honest as I believed he could be with me for quite some time following this day. I struggled with my inner depression daily and continued to struggle to eat. Alen avoided Mara's phone calls and even though he worked with his father, he avoided talking to him as much as possible even while at work, from what he told me. We had conversations and I was no longer alone with my thoughts. Although we couldn't be free to travel and be spontaneous as we had a mortgage, car payment and work, we did have times when we would simply be together and enjoy whatever little moments we could create. One day road trips were welcome. Dinner dates and movie nights were a treat. We began to live. Mara and Kreso were now part of our past and they finally stopped trying to call as we never picked up.

After what I felt was a life I could live with and eventually would find my way back to happiness, *I was happy enough*. Alen and I seemed to be having a normal, regular life and I grew to accept this. This was now my life, our life and we would be ok. Alen and I agreed that we would start our family. It didn't take long at all to become pregnant with our son after our decision was made. It felt like time to begin our family. I was feeling better with Kreso and Mara now out of our lives and Alen was standing firm with his will to break the bond. I was finally feeling joy, knowing I was becoming a Mom and would soon welcome our baby boy. Alen and I talked about baby names and I was thrilled we had narrowed it down to a couple we both liked. Everything would be ok now. I was still tired and hungry, but I was grateful again.

I AM Lucy

*The only time my kids got to be kids were at my parent's home.
They didn't even know it but Baka Anica and Dida Đuka were God sends.*

13 PART THIRTEEN
2005 CONRICH, CANADA
FINALLY, I FELL APART

"*No!* You can't make him leave! Bring him back *now!*" I demanded of the Nurse whose attention I now had in the palm of my hand. She seemed to ignore me until now. Now she was listening! Now I had her attention! Now she heard me and I saw it in her eyes. She was teetering between what to make of it, abuse or true love? Which was it? I quickly had to reassure her that the choice was clear.

"He's the only one who can calm me down! He's my rock!" I cried. Then, I switched into the quiet, calming voice that Alen proved to me, time and again, helped everyone listen and feel reassured no matter how obvious the situation had been, no matter how terrible, that he was telling the truth and was to be trusted. "I need him here. *Please.*"

I knew she had taken another peak at my vitals. She was well aware of my heart rate and blood pressure which were so high at first, now slowing down as I breathed slowly and quietly as I reassured her that I needed him, please. I learned techniques to help me remain calm in many stressful situations to keep myself safe for the past several years. Breathe. Hush. Those things I once did to simply reset myself to enjoy life had now become lifesaving. Slow it down. Think of beaches and the sea and the scent of Ivankovo. Think of the ladies on the bench, inviting me to sit and chat. Yes, breathe, hush myself, relax. Everything was now alright. I controlled my breathing, controlled my heart and mind.

As my heart rate decreased and my blood pressure lowered, the performance was now over and would have won me yet another academy award, in my own world. I was feeling clearer, more awake than when Alen and I had left our house. I was feeling fear again, regardless of the comfort Alen brought me at home. I was back and forth in my mind, feeling fear and panic then feeling reassured that I was simply insane. I had such a supportive husband, such a caring man. I was once so terrified of him, ungrateful, now I needed him and I needed his forgiveness for being such a bad person all those years. Whatever the truth, I needed him back in my hospital room before he doubted my loyalty to him. The Nurse turned to the door, opened it and seconds later Alen walked back in.

I scanned his face. His skin tone for color. *Was he red, neutral or pale?* Neutral. *Were his eyes light, dark, have they turned yellowish green or were they crystal clear and practically see through and piercing?* Somewhat lighter than usual, but they weren't glowing, good. Eyebrows? *Were they resting peacefully or joining? Were they raised in question or frowning? Any anger or disappointment?* Slightly raised but the look he always gave of innocence. Good. *Any veins pulsing?* I scanned for the swelling of veins, above his eyebrow, neck, arms, hands. Nothing. Again, good. *Any glisten of sweat?* His skin was dry, no sign of sweat so I must have been fast enough. Good. I had hope. *Were his lips open or closed?* Closed. This wasn't good, they should be slightly open, not showing any teeth but still, slightly open. Possible problem. I searched his jaw line to see if he was clenching his teeth or relaxed? Okay, some relief now as he wasn't clenching. Good. Quickly I scanned his posture. *Where were his shoulders?* Somewhat hunched but not overly. Good. *Was his back straight or bent?* Slightly bent giving good reason for the positioning of his shoulders but not an alarm. A bit relaxed. Good. *Where were his arms?* They were loosely by his side, one slightly more forward than the other. Slight bend at the elbow, no tension. Good. *Were his hands loose or in a fist, was he rubbing any fingers together?* All good. Hands unclenched. Right hand, fidgeting a bit so he's only a little nervous. He's not angry, just a bit nervous. Good.

This scan had only taken me seconds to complete at any given time. Seconds to scan for all the signs and I knew, regardless of the muscle relaxant that began to flow into my veins from the IV the Nurse poked into me earlier, I made it in good time after all. I had less than 30 seconds to get him back into the hospital room with me in order for him to be reassured that I didn't say anything negative about him to anyone. That I didn't let them know that I was in trouble. That I hadn't given anyone *any* reason to believe he shouldn't be trusted or admired. My scan told me I made it in time, but he was still standing. *Why was he still standing?*

Maybe I missed something! The scan passed and he should be sitting. He was still standing! Oh Lord I missed something. Then, the Nurse returned and offered us both a warm blanket. Yes! I passed with flying colors after all. Alen smiled and looked toward me, letting me know all was now as it should be and he was calm. He wouldn't have to tell Kreso and Mara to begin the process of taking my kids away for good. He wouldn't send them any alarms, any red flags, I was safe. My kids were safe. He sat. Thank God, he sat. And the Nurse did even better than I would have hoped for when she offered him that warm blanket. Proving to him, he was now very safe and in turn, I was safe. My head fell to the pillow and I breathed so deeply, as a warmth flowed through my veins taking over my entire body.

"You should now be feeling much calmer, more relaxed." The Nurse explained quietly while looking towards me. "You gave all of us quite a scare." She reassured me with a giggle that sounded like a song, gently being sung to me as I still struggled to stay awake. I wanted to hear more. I didn't want them to talk alone. But I achieved what I needed to do, now maybe I could accept I should rest a bit. Maybe I could simply enjoy this wonderful feeling taking over me, as the change in my body filled me with warmth, almost like ten warm blankets were now hugging me gently, rocking me to sleep. Wonderful. How wonderful this feeling was.

As I slowly slipped into a beautiful peace, I listened as she explained to Alen what the Doctor had determined and what treatment they were administering to me. He listened intently, I'm sure the Nurse imagined he was so worried for me. I desperately wanted to be with my kids. I had to do things I hated, no one would understand. I had to. But they wouldn't understand. No one would ever understand. *How could they?* I hardly understood myself. As I now heard only bits of what was being said and my mind seemed foggier than earlier that day, during the end of Kreso and Mara's visit, I still clung to hear the words, listen to tones, assess the vibration in the room. I thought of how crazy I must be. Alen said he was with us during their visit and that I said yes to them. I was in love with Alen, *why had I feared him moments ago?* I was awful, such an awful person.

"We've actually never seen anything like it before, which is why we assumed her brain was hemorrhaging. So sorry for the scare but really, all of her symptoms indicated a brain hemorrhage." The Nurse continued to tell him that after tests came back and the Doctor assessed me, they were now confident that my brain was alright but that my mind was not. "I've been at this for many years and have never seen anyone with such a severe reaction to stress. The Neurologist is definitely going to have a follow up with your wife and is quite alarmed with the level of stress she's showing." She said quietly.

Although I was now falling even further into a drugged state, I listened to her every word so I could make sure Alen was still ok. I remembered some, putting words together at times. I knew she explained that I would need serious help. Alen reassured her that he understood what she was saying. He explained that as I lay there, slipping away, I had suffered for many years with internal battles that he just couldn't seem to help me with, no matter how hard he tried. He was so dedicated, so in love. His heart was breaking to see me like this. He had loved me since he was four years old. Soul mates. The Nurse explained that they were going to leave my care to Alen now as obviously, him and I had a great bond, a beautiful relationship…. He was my rock… He promised to take me to a Doctor later in the week…. He fully understood how serious this was and would do anything to help me…. He may even get help himself as this was so stressful for him as well and had been going on for so long….. He would ensure our kids weren't affected…. Sleep took me away and I dreamed many, beautiful, dreams. For the first time in years, I was dreaming.

When I awoke, we were at home and I was back on the couch. *How? When?* It didn't even matter. I remembered my last vision of Alen still there in his chair, in the Hospital room with the blanket hugging his lap. He was treated well. Just as he had been through both of our kids' births. Alen was cared for far better than even I was through both labors. I made sure of it. I made sure to tell Nurses of how loving, caring and devoted of a man he was. If everyone showered Alen with attention, admiration, envy, I was left in peace. I was safe.

During our son's birth, the Nurses loved Alen so much they brought in a lazy boy and several warm blankets for him. They brought him coffee and juice, while I simply waited out my contractions. As long as Alen felt loved by the world I was ok, I was at peace. I didn't need the attention. Even during each contraction as he giggled from the comfort of his lazy boy, telling me to hang on, push through, we're almost there! Even when I was crying inside, after realizing Alen named our Son and even decided the spelling would be unique, I remained calm and focused on everyone believing we shared this too. A name we hadn't discussed at all. A name that wasn't part of the couple we both agreed on through my pregnancy. A name that was his Father's, the English version of Kresimir. Kristopher. Of course I loved my own Son's name and cherished it just as much as Alen, Kreso and Mara had. Of course. What's a name anyway, I thought. I have a Son, that's what's most important.

Then, 20 months later during our Daughter's birth, same scenario. Again, I now had a Daughter, what could be more important than this? Nothing. He named her and I agreed. Even though again, we had narrowed it down the month before her birth. Even though he gave me that false sense of being part of a decision, again. I have a Daughter, that's what's most important.

Then, the decision that Alen and I would only have two children as Mara insisted that two was enough. Of course this was alright with me too. Why would I ever want to bring more children into this clan, this group, this insanity? I was silly, stupid forever thinking I would want to have so many children. Two was perfect. Yes, I would learn to accept that even though the love I had for my two beautiful babies erased all else in my awful world, I wouldn't bring any more into it.

How did we get home? Last I recalled, seeing Alen covered with a blanket as I drifted away, I knew the Nurse believed every word I tried to say before the muscle relaxant took over. I knew that even I believed some of what I said. It was real and I made it in time. It was coming back to me, when the Nurse had asked Alen to leave after putting my IV in, the muscle relaxant to help relax my body, my mind. She questioned me about our relationship and stated they were highly concerned with the level of stress I showed and that Alen was the cause. That he was abusing me. That I needed help. She was not only completely correct, I could add two more people to the list that finally broke me and brought me to this condition.

Around 24 hours earlier, my mind finally broke. I believe I felt it break. If a mind could be shattered, mine was in pieces. It had enough and couldn't take any more. I felt it. I must have slipped away, in and out of consciousness maybe? I could hardly remember the drive to the walk-in clinic, I definitely couldn't remember the drive to the hospital. I remembered how thoughtful Alen was, his smile, his laugh. I remembered that at the clinic, the Doctor wanted to call an ambulance to take me to the Foothills Hospital as she believed my brain was hemorrhaging, but Alen insisted he would drive me instead. He seemed confident, knowing I would be alright. The Doctor wasn't nearly as sure as he was. I couldn't remember the drive. *Why couldn't I remember this drive? Maybe 911 was called after all? When had I called my parents?* I knew they were there, at the Hospital to take my kids. They took them, they would be safe. *But when did I call them? Did I call them?* Alen must have called them, he was kind and thoughtful that way, wasn't he? *Where were my kids while we drove?* They must have been so scared. Maybe not. Maybe I'd remember soon. Yes, I'd remember. I was still just so sleepy.

Now I wondered, when were Kreso and Mara with me at my house having that awful coffee she made? I still tasted the bitterness, she must have forgotten I took it with sugar, both times she made it. I tried to remember what happened during this visit, this visit that was another task, another duty I had to perform. *Was that yesterday? Last week? Why was my head so foggy? Where was Alen? He was there, wasn't he? Why couldn't I remember where he sat? Did he say anything at all?*

I focused. Their visit, regardless of when it happened, this is when my mind started to shatter, I thought. I felt it when Kreso and Mara sat in front of me, in my home, while Alen was at work and my kids were taking their nap. No, he was there. He said he was. *What did he say?* Oh how I wished I could just remember! We sat, drinking the coffee. This was new. I remembered she scolded me when I wouldn't take the coffee and she insisted I do and that it would help me wake up. She said I looked awful. I looked tired. I was obviously weak. How would I even think to care for my kids in this condition, she sneered. Yes, of course I drank her coffee. Protect my kids. Wake up. Look alive. *What would people think?* Had I known what this day would bring, had I realized that this was yet another new path to the absolute end of me, would I have had the strength to lock the door?

This was the start of yet another normal part of life I wouldn't question. For years to come, following this very day, Mara would begin to bring her own food, make her own coffee, and we would all eat only her food and her drinks, while she stated she simply knew I couldn't do anything well enough. At the time, I would have no way of knowing that for years to come, Mara would do all the cooking when we were together and would always insist that she didn't need my help. She would tell me to buy cookbooks and learn to finally cook and, in the meantime, she would take care of everything. I was useless in her eyes and she couldn't believe that a woman at my age was so awful at being a wife and Mom.

Yes, eat her food and drink her coffee. I would understand that this kept her from taking my kids. *Maybe I wasn't a good Mom after all?* I was so tired all the time, this wasn't safe for my kids, was it? I no longer would offer my help and would stay out of the kitchen to allow her the space she needed to create her masterpieces, always followed with serving that bitter coffee she so loved to make. Alen and Kreso never complained about the taste, the after taste or the bitterness. They seemed to enjoy it. I grew to need it. Eventually, I would request it. The day would come where I would even ask her to make it and I would welcome her visit, looking forward to her meals and yes, the bitter coffee I grew to want, to need. The day would come when I would be completely ignorant to this process, this development, this necessity. But this day, I only tried to understand where my memory had gone. Trying to fill in the missing pieces of the puzzle, yet some pieces were taken away and hidden underground. Far beneath the surface. One day, I would dig them up and find them, I thought. One day, I would find each missing piece. I was just tired. I should be so grateful to these people who took me in, regardless of how stupid and weak I was. Yes, I would be thankful.

This day, as I sipped on the bitter coffee, Kreso demanded I take on and sue the large oil company on his behalf. The year before I had taken on the same type of case on Alen's behalf. An impossible battle, but I won. The Lawyer insisted when I convinced him to take on the case and that I would do most of the work that there was no way to win. The large oil company was a multi billion-dollar company with top lawyers and limitless funds. None of this scared me, I had far worse people to deal with. I was not intimidated by the large oil company, I feared three people who made it clear they could take my kids away, forever. As Alen had been let go from the very same company his father worked for, it would make sense that I should now take his father's case on as well. His father was the Vice President, Alen had been a Millwright. When Alen was let go, he insisted his name and reputation be saved and that I had to save it. He insisted that the people at the large oil company were wrong to let him go and they would have to pay for this and apologize to him for their mistreatment. Against my morals, my very being, everything that I managed to hold on to and believed still made me somewhat a decent person, I did as I was told in order to be with my kids. Alen promised he would never again ask me for another favor. Alen promised but that, to me, meant nothing. What meant something was that I promised myself. That meant everything. I would never again do anything against my nature. Never again.

Although I wasn't allowed to continue my education after marriage, Alen knew I was smart. Alen knew I could talk to Presidents and Lawyers and all educated elite in his world and never embarrass him. He knew I didn't need a formal education to perform as though I had one. He would use this to his advantage for years to come. He would use me to win lawsuits, win friends, win admiration from the ladies, build a successful business and even afford him the freedom to take trips on his own and continue to enjoy life like he never had before. He gained his freedom from the chains that once held him down. *Alen was free.* Alen became the free spirit while I became his accountant, his lawyer, his project manager, his liaison, his banker, his scapegoat, his everything.

I would know how to solve everything. I made anything he asked of me happen. He knew he could set out to do anything, accomplish anything as all he simply had to do is tell me to make it happen, and I would. I made all his wishes and his dreams come to life, regardless of how difficult they may have been or how impossible they seemed to be. *I had to have my children!* Nothing would ever be too impossible for me to accomplish as I had the biggest motivation a person could have.

Had I known that the years to follow this very day I would turn into a machine, a wonderful supportive machine, I would have locked the front door and never allowed Kreso and Mara in. Why hadn't I locked the door? Why hadn't I taken my kids and fled? *And do what? And go where?* After so many years, try to explain to those I lied to for so long, that I was actually terrified of these people? The very people that whenever we were in public, I presented to be almost worthy of Heaven's praise? Impossible! No one would believe me now and even if they did, they would blame me as I blamed myself. No, I wouldn't have been able to lock the door. I never could.

I did everything for Alen. I found a Lawyer and all communication with the Lawyer was on me. Every time the Lawyer said we needed to give up I would sit and write pages to prove why we had to keep going. I made the phone calls, answered all questions. All the while the Lawyer understood that Alen was far too busy with work and caring for our kids. All the while, really, Alen went out drinking and enjoying his life. Alen never cared for our kids. Alen spent many nights out, not coming home. All the while Alen threatened that if I should lose the lawsuit, he would have no choice but to unleash his father and mother and leave with my children as he would have no reason to stay. I would be of no use to him or my kids. He would have to ensure everyone knew I was to blame for his job loss and he would simply tell everyone it was me who brought him to failure. He had no choice but to save himself and his children from *me*.

When Alen wasn't threatening to take my kids, he was threatening suicide. Yes, the suicide threats began around this time. During the time of Alen's lawsuit against the large oil company. They came alive again full force and worse than ever before. Then to add to all of this, throughout this lawsuit, Kreso and Mara demanded I quit the lawsuit as it was affecting Kreso who still worked for the large oil company. What a mess of a situation I was in. Trying to keep all three happy, Alen, Kreso and Mara, was almost impossible, but I eventually succeeded, and in the end, I still had my kids with me. Kreso at one point even tried to bribe me, offering me $25,000 cash if I would drop the case Alen wanted me to win. I knew Kreso would never have actually given me $25k, it was only a way to have Alen be angry with me. Another way to interfere and ensure I was always on my toes. Insanity. It was all simply insane. I would battle myself trying to figure the three of them out, who was following who's orders. It seemed to always change and I could never keep up. In the end, I won the case for Alen, I won. I won to ensure Alen wouldn't allow Kreso and Mara to take my kids away.

The day Kreso and Mara sat in front of me, in my home, Kreso explained he was being let go from the large oil company and he set out to punish them. Who were they to make such a bad decision? Did they not know who he was? Did they not know how important he had been to the company? Did they not know that he was the only money maker in the entire place? That without him, they would be nothing? That without him, no one would even want to stay employed there? Apparently not, as he was served with papers and now sat, with his devoted and well-presented wife beside him always, instructing me on how I was to get a lawyer, sue the large oil company, and win. Just as I had for Alen. Otherwise, they would make my life hell, again.

My mind was spinning. My stomach now had a constant burn that never went away. It was simply a constant. I hardly ever even noticed it.

"No," I said. I had a simple response and I meant it. No. I wouldn't do this and I couldn't do this. Mara got up and made coffee a second time. I refused her offer but she insisted. She was easily angered and if I didn't agree or follow her demands quickly, she would glare with hatred and then simply look toward Kreso, reminding me that she was in control of him, he was in control of me. This was just how things worked. Or, did this not happen at all? Was I dreaming? Oh how I wanted to sleep.

Each time I was instructed on yet another mission, so to speak, it was to save my life from hell. If I didn't do as I was told, Alen would then suffer which meant my kids would then suffer and in turn, I would suffer. Simple. When they wanted to make my life hell, they simply either stated they would begin the process to take my kids away or went through Alen to ensure he made me suffer. It had been going on since our son's birth and hadn't stopped, it only worsened with time. As Alen had recently made the decision to leave his current employer to start his own company, without any input from me, of course, I was already going through an immense amount of stress as I knew, debt would now be a permanent part of our lives and more secrets were being created. Alen wouldn't have to deal with the debt, but I would. I was the accountant, the banker. I was always spending very little and had to watch pennies so to speak. I was always the lowest on this totem pole the Trio created within their own minds, within their family. The three of them. That was all that ever mattered.

Some wondered why Alen's only brother would end up being so ill, dying inside, so quiet himself. They would wonder, but I knew. I saw. I replaced him in a way and I understood. Alen's brother hardly existed in this world of three, being a fourth member. Being the one ignored or broken. The one accused then becoming a martyr. The one who had a soul, who didn't fit the mold. Exiled. Yet they still controlled him, even though he wanted out and they too wanted him out, they would drag him back in whenever they felt the need to use him. Everyone can be used, everyone had a purpose, family was no exception. If you didn't serve a purpose for the three Trio, either you didn't exist or you risked becoming a target for them to shoot. They had no boundaries for even their own, much less for me or those who came into their lives.

So, I said no to Kreso and as Kreso and Mara sat in front of me, staring as though they had never heard such a word be used before, I repeated, "no." I was sure of my decision! I was done with them and I was done doing anything for them. I had my kids to worry about. I had Alen to now think about with the new company coming and I had no idea what it all even involved, but I was sure I would have more duties added to my daily tasks and another lawsuit, for them, was not an option. Alen would have to agree as he should be my priority. I would convince him that he was my everything and taking his parents' case on would distract me from helping him.

Kreso glared at me as I took another sip of the coffee Mara handed me. I had seen this glare once before, the day I returned home in 2001, after fleeing with my baby boy for the first time when he was just under a year old, not realizing I was already pregnant with my second child. That day when he became so irate, he put his own head through the wall in our Beddington home as I stood inches away holding our son, trying my best to protect us both from his rage.

Running to my friend Karla's house once I was able to escape, I told her everything. This would be the first of many times I fled, and it would be the last time I spoke the truth to anyone about my fear or of my escapes. I told her how terrified I was as I tried to remain calm for my son. I stayed there for a bit then went to my parent's home and eventually, I returned to Alen accepting his apology and his promises, once again.

When I returned home Kreso was there as well, waiting with what I felt to be the closest to a death glare I ever encountered. Kreso this day stared at me with hatred. Kreso spoke very slowly, clearly and in a stern, angry tone, warning me that if I were to ever leave with Alen's son again, he would take every measure to ensure I never saw my son again. He reminded me he had millions in the bank.

He reminded me he had influential friends. He reminded me he had power. He made it very clear that I was to be at home, beside my husband, no matter what. *No matter what.*

He stated that Alen simply put his head through the wall because I made him angry. I had to work on never making Alen angry again and this was part of my duty as a wife. He stated that Alen hurt his own head, not mine. He said I should accept that I was lucky that Alen cared for me, saving me from harm and only hurting himself. He explained this would never happen again and that Alen had every right to hurt me if I angered him, not himself.

He said all of this with Alen right beside him. Alen sat silent and listened to his father's words as though he heard them before. He didn't argue them or acknowledge them, he simply allowed them to be spoken. And now, this day, as Kreso and Mara sat in front of me, I saw the very same glare, the same hatred. I already knew what Kreso was going to say, and he did. Threatening me with the most calm and terrifying look, he would take both my children away and ensure I am left not just homeless, but hopeless. He informed me that I would never, ever see my children again and he would ensure they would grow up hating me.

Kreso rose and Mara immediately followed. He turned to me one last time before leaving my house and said, "You might think you can say no to me, but you can't. You *will* do this. You *will* win for me. Or you *will* lose everything you love." With that, he looked toward my children's bedroom door where they lay sleeping, then left. Mara right at his feet.

When did Alen come home? Was it later that night? Right after Kreso and Mara had left? Was he there during their visit after all? I couldn't recall at all when Alen simply showed up. I do remember though that I told him I had already called my parents and they were aware that I was unwell. This was my safeguard, my way of telling him he couldn't win, not this time. I also told him that my parents knew to expect my call and that they would care for the kids. If they didn't get my call I was certain they would simply come looking for me.

Alen's expression was different, almost humorous. He was smiling. How odd, I thought. He was happy? He sat with me and wasn't angry. I was so confused! I couldn't think straight but I knew well enough this would be something to naturally set Alen in a rage and even cause him to punch walls and shout. But there he was, he was calm and almost happy. He sat, watching me as I sat silent, watching him. Something was so different, I thought. *What was going on?*

My mind was giving up and I knew this, I was aware. I was thirsty and looked down and saw my cup, only a small amount left from what Mara had made for me during their awful visit. He saw this and lifted the cup for me, offering it to me. I drank the rest, still watching him closely as something, there was definitely something, so different today. Although I wanted to understand what was really happening to Alen, I was letting go, losing myself.

"Shhh." He quietly hushed me, even though I wasn't speaking. "It's all going to be ok now." He whispered. My heart raced and I was struggling to get up, I needed to move away from him but I couldn't. I lied down, feeling as though a weight was pushing me further and further, how much further could I go? *Was I lying down yet?*

"What's going on?" I cried. I couldn't move but no one was holding me down. He kept looking at me and reassured me that all would be alright, nothing was wrong and that I shouldn't be frightened. My lips started to quiver, then suddenly went into a spasm. I could no longer control my lips, my face, my eyebrows. Everything started to move all on its own. *What was happening?!* My head began to jerk. I lost all control of myself! My neck sent my head to the left so fast, then snapped back into place as though an elastic band lost the battle and was cut in half. Again and again my head did this awful, uncontrollable jerk. *What was happening to me?*

Alen smiled again and called to the children to get ready to leave and that they would have to take Mom to the Doctor. I had no idea how long I had been lying there, helpless. It could have been minutes, hours or even a day. I had no idea. He reassured them that I would be fine and not to worry. I simply wasn't feeling well. This was the very first time Alen offered to take me to a Doctor and although I wouldn't know it then, it would also be the last. Something was definitely wrong. All I could think was to call my parents. I tried to plead with Alen to call them, but he wouldn't. I couldn't move. He smiled and said all would be ok and not to worry.

Was my face simply normal? Why did I feel the movements forcing my head to make sudden jerks? Where was Alen? I panicked and felt alone. My heart raced but then slowed again, I felt sick. He brought me a glass of water which I somehow managed to drink all at once. I didn't care I was spilling, I needed water desperately. I spoke, I think. I tried telling him I refused to help his parents. I tried telling him I said no! He laughed and said that in fact, I told his parents yes, and that he was there for the entire visit. He told me I accepted the case and that I would win. I had no options, I would do as I was told.

My world was crashing and I could hardly breathe. I was now in a true panic. He reassured me, reminded me to take slow, deep breaths. He told me that what I was going through was simply a fight within myself. I had to simply accept that I was a good person now, wanting to help his parents and see that everything in my past was wrong, so wrong. He was so relieved for me as I had suffered for too many years, blaming him. I was finally becoming a good person and my conscious was simply going through an internal battle between good and bad.

I needed more water, I begged him for more water. I drank more and listened. Words were coming and going and I had little use for understanding them. I no longer questioned them, I simply accepted they were so reassuring, so calm, so right. I heard them. I began to understand them. Somehow, I began to calm down as I heard him repeat such calming words and all was going to be ok.

When I was able to move again, I brought my legs off the couch and with his help, I stood and was ready to walk. He held me, he was my support. He reassured me that all was going to be ok now. He would get me to a Doctor and everything would be okay. He even brought me the phone so I could finally call my parents. Oh how I was so grateful to him. I couldn't remember their phone number so he kindly dialed for me, passing me the phone. How wonderful, I thought. How could I have ever hated him? Feared him? He was really there for me, supporting me, what a wonderful man. Although I wasn't quite sure what I was saying to my parents, I did remember I made them promise to keep my kids safe and that I would be okay, I just wasn't feeling well but not to worry, Alen was really helping me and I would be okay. I wanted to tell them more, that something was *really wrong* and that I felt Kreso and Mara had something to do with it, but I couldn't. I only managed to tell them to keep my children safe, then again, my mind was clouded and memory began to fade away again.

14 PART FOURTEEN

2007
THE LIFE I WAS SHOWN TO LIVE

Life had a way of moving on. Regardless of my guilt for treating Alen, Chris and Mara so poorly the years before. Regardless of how selfish I had once been. There were some days when I felt I had a right to fear them, to hate them. Thankfully these feelings quickly left me, not lasting longer than hours at most, any given occurrence.

I now had an incredible ability to work 12, 16, sometimes up to 36 hours straight and feel zero fogginess or fatigue. I simply refused to rest until all of my duties were complete, or at least enough for the time being that is. Then, reset and continue with my duties again. Duties were a constant. Always so much to get done and I was the only one who could do them. For the most part, I was able to outperform even Alen's most cherished employees and still made zero errors, needed very little sleep and always, always had my children with me. They were my inspiration! They were my everything. I loved them and was thankful each day, each hour, each minute that I was with them. There would be times when I would wish I could simply take them to a park, to soccer games or even to the zoo! Oh this would be wonderful, I thought. But no. I was so grateful that I could just be with them for now. If I worked hard enough I would earn some free time with them. I would get to take them places and explore. The day would come, I was sure of it, when we would have some free time to enjoy.

I was no longer that selfish, argumentative person I once had been. I was no longer that irresponsible, miserable person, she no longer existed! Thank goodness! I was so fortunate. My mind must have abandoned most memories from the past to safeguard me from relapse. To save me from being so confused with the Trio, who I was sure at some point, I must have treated terribly. They were gracious enough to never speak of it, of my mistreatment toward them. This allowed me to move forward and be a role model for my children.

Work hard, ensure they went to school and succeeded and followed the rules. Never, ever to question Alen as he was so unbelievably talented, so smart, so giving. Always to remember, that without Alen, Kreso and Mara, we would have nothing. They worked so hard to provide, they must have worked even harder to accept me. I would always be grateful I was allowed to have my children. One day, I knew my kids would understand why the sacrifices we made for the family were needed. One day they would understand that these sacrifices were needed for the opportunities Alen had in life. They would one day be ours to enjoy as well, once we earned them. Once I worked hard enough. They were how we would one day be free. This would be how we would get to have free time and maybe, just maybe even go on a trip.

My son's first day of Kindergarten was so exciting! I prepared him so long for this day to come. The rewards of education. The rewards of excelling within society and how important it was to become a part of it. Kris seemed not to believe me as much as Mia had, but I was sure he would come around. He had to. It was simply the way things worked. He would accept it and would love it, I was sure of this. Alen reminded us often of why I was unable to make a living. Why I had to keep working for nothing. He would explain to the kids that I had no education. I was stupid in the eyes of society. I was useless to them. I would never really succeed. No one would hire me and I had no skills. Our children deserved more and needed to succeed in school. They needed to strive to be nothing like me, their Mom.

As I drove to the school, I spoke of these things and reminded Kris of the importance of this day. Reassuring him that he would now finally begin a wonderful journey and become a member of society for the first time, while his little sister only wished she too could join him in this wonderful new journey. Mia was envious of Kris's first day of school and wished she could go along. Why she had to wait another year frustrated her but she would patiently await her turn. Kris was quiet yet reassured me he would be alright.

"Of course you'll be alright," I smiled. Why wouldn't he be? I thought. I peeked at him through my rear-view mirror, his eyes had a slight glisten. Tears? "Be strong Kris, you know what Tata says about tears." He smiled, reassuring me that he was alright. His eyes, still glistening.

"I know Mom. I love you," he said.

Arriving at the school in Chestermere, we found our way to the grassy patch just outside the Kindergarten entrance. This was nice, I thought, they had a separate entrance for such little people. Wonderful. My little boy wouldn't have to get squished between all those teenagers, he would be safe. Mia was beyond excited for her brother and was talking to him of this great beginning, this great day he was now able to be part of society and prove he belonged. Oh how we had talked about this day with Alen many, many times in preparation. Kris stood by me, quietly listening to his sister and assured her he heard every word and was thankful to her for such support.

My kids were amazing little people. They weren't like the others I now watched running around us, shouting, screeching, playing tag. No, they were responsible and very respectful of their surroundings and of others. They had spent the past year with me at work, helping me run a business and proved to everyone they were respectful, mature and understood how important cooperation was to a good life. They knew how to behave according to Alen's rules and those rules, we all understood, were what made Alen such a well respected and admired man. Yes, these two little people were far beyond these other children who obviously didn't understand that without hard work, without a serious take on life, there was nothing. How would these other children ever grow to be responsible adults? How would they accept the awful and scary world out there, the real world. The world that is always out to get us? I had pity for these children. They would be so saddened one day to see they were so unprepared.

The school bell rang and my heart suddenly raced. I felt a rush of heat stream through my chest, neck and into my face. I felt so panicked. *Oh God! What was I doing? Why were we here? Why am I forcing my son to think this was a great journey?* I couldn't think. I couldn't understand why these thoughts now rushed at me. This was so wrong! But why? I looked to Kris and his eyes glistened even more, while his smile still reassured me all would be okay. He held my hand, his tiny hand so full of love, full of comfort.

"It's okay Mom. You'll be okay." I bent down to hug him and thanked him. He always knew, somehow, he always knew how I felt. Always. He reassured me that I would be okay. Why would he say that? He hugged me and whispered his encouraging words once more, then slowly walked toward that awful door that was held open by some stern looking woman who would now control my son. My poor son. Why was I letting him go? Why hadn't I wiped away his tears? I knew I couldn't. I shouldn't. Why was I feeling so terrible?

As I stood staring off at what was now a closed, locked door surrounded by silence, Mia called out to me to wake me from my pain. I felt as though I had just abandoned my son for the first time. I knew I had disappointed him before, not sure when, but I had. I was sure of it. But this feeling was new to me. This would be the first time I felt I truly abandoned him. It wouldn't be the last. I felt as though I released him into a wild kingdom, where vultures and lions roamed free. I felt as though I failed him. I had no idea why. These were just, feelings. Feelings that made no sense. Feelings that were so strong, without reason.

I drove to work with Mia strapped into her seat, nice and safe as always, and searched for Alen as soon as we arrived. Mia, always my perfect little angel and knowing what needed to be done at all times and now nearly 4 years old, immediately found her seat and began to scribble in her book. Quiet, she was now to remain quiet and proper. She knew, she understood that Alen approved of her proper, polite, lady like presence. She knew, without him ever having to say a word to acknowledge it, that she was being good. She followed the rules. She played her part.

I explained to Alen immediately what I experienced at the school. This was always how I reset myself from a panic. I didn't have them as often as before, but they still came about and caught me off guard each time. Talk to Alen. I would always know I had to talk to Alen as soon as they hit.

"Never let them last long", he would remind me. "You could slip away for good this time," he would warn. There were times when some unexplained feeling, some strange panic would rush at me. I knew, as Alen had explained so many times already, this was still part of the awful mental breakdown I experienced and I simply had to seek his advice to move forward. I needed his guidance, his reassurance. My memories of years ago must have played some role in it, and only Alen was ever able to reassure me and bring me back to calm. He would remind me not to talk to anyone else about these episodes as they would worry for me. They would think I was still as unstable as I had been. They wouldn't understand. They would look at me differently. He would remind me to be happy with this new self of mine, keep moving forward. He would remind me that the evil that used to consume me simply wanted to return. I needed to push it back! Ignore it!

Fight to stay in the present and not allow the evil to take me again.

So today, he reassured me that it was my mind simply playing games with me once again. I needed to remain strong and not allow the children to see any sign that I was frail. If I explored these feelings of panic, I could be lost forever. I could lose my mind, forever. What an awful thought. Terrifying! One of the very few memories I could recall from my break down, was how awful and terrifying it was to have no control over my mind and body. If it were to happen again, I would be gone forever. He would question me, *who would then take care of the kids?* He would have no choice but to have Mara raise them. He would have no choice as she was at home full time, had the financial ability and she had successfully raised him. Yes, this would be the only choice, I agreed. It pained me, but I agreed.

"Do you need a sip?" He asked me, eyebrows slightly raised with concern.

"Oh no, I'm okay. Thank you though. I'm fine now." I reassured him that all would be okay. I had control again. I didn't want a sip of the syrup he had in the desk. It was awful, it was so bitter. Yes, it would make everything go away but then I would miss most of the day. I would forget. I would have to push my panic away on my own. There were times when I couldn't and taking the sip was necessary. He kept this medicine from me as he said he feared I may take it without his knowledge. I may take too much. Taking it was like erasing hours of my present life. Not only would I forget my panic, I would have no idea what I had done that very day and would be missing it, gone from memory, for good. No. I didn't need it, not today. I wanted to remember picking Kris up from school and hear of his first day at school. I wanted to remember this and keep it forever. I wanted some memories I could cling to. This day would be good.

I regained control of my mind and breathed deeply, resetting my heart rate and bringing myself back in the now. There was a lot of work to be done, as was every day. I had been working full time now, helping Alen's company, helping Alen. He was too important to be bothered with most of the menial tasks so I was always there, helping. I had been the one to solve the first near miss with payroll during the first month of opening the business.

What a relief I was there shortly after their start up, stopping only for a visit, yet Alen and his partner brought me quickly into an office to tell me of his partner's mistake. They needed $30,000.00 by next day. Yes, next day. Payroll could not be missed yet they had neglected to invoice some customers, which meant, they were now short $30,000.00 for payroll, tomorrow. They looked at me, Alen was angry. I suggested they simply explain to the guys that payroll would be late and rush an invoice to their customer. This was not an option and one that forced Alen to demand his partner leave the office in order for him to scold me for thinking of such a useless solution. Alen explained to me that had I not been at home with my kids, they wouldn't be missing payroll. Had I cared at all for him, I would have been there to ensure this never happened. Had I not been so consumed with those children, he wouldn't be in such a mess today. He instructed me to form a proper solution and I only had less than an hour to do so. I quickly scanned my thoughts for solutions.

I made a call to a friend in Bowden. A businessman who hired Alen to rebuild an injector for him the year before and I helped the entire process right from home. A businessman who, through this rebuild, I developed a solid and working relation with regardless of my zero experience with the oilfield, the industry. This was my duty, my part in keeping my family together. Always ensure a good, solid and profitable relation with everyone, at all times. Ensure Alen would be able to use them in the future, as there was always a time he would need something, from someone, somewhere. I called Bowden and buried any dignity I had, I needed to save Alen, to save my family. I needed to keep us together. To keep my children. Alen stared at me in awe as I spoke on the phone. He himself was surprised at my choice to call Bowden. Who had he expected me to call? I had a list in my mind, but who would he have thought should be first? Looking at his expression, I knew he had no thoughts of who to call at all. He was clueless. I quickly ignored this and continued to solve the problem. This was why he needed me so much. This was why I knew, somewhere deep within me, that as long as he needed me, as long as I was useful, I would have my family, my children.

The conversation was quick. My friend questioned how such a mistake could happen and insisted this was not good business, he feared I was mixed into a situation that would become bankrupt in no time. He was unimpressed with Alen and his partner already after meeting with them shortly after the business opened. I quickly reassured him that this was my error. I had made the mistake and this was why I had to also solve it. This, within seconds, resulted in my friend from Bowden coming through and telling me I could drive up at once and pick up the cheque. He said this with one condition, that as long as it was me who came in person. He would not give this cheque to anyone else. He would not loan it to anyone else, only to me. I thanked him and offered $2,000 as an interest payment to ensure it was understood I practiced good business. I understood my request was short notice and he was helping me out with a $30,000.00-dollar cheque within hours. He appreciated this and agreed, this was now good business.

I ended the phone call knowing I had very little time to not only drive up to Bowden but reach the bank before it closed for the day in order to ensure full payroll would be covered through the night. Alen was suddenly irate. He grabbed his stapler and whipped it across the office. The action and loud bang startled me and I jumped back.

"You just throw money away like that so *easy* don't you?" He growled. "Must be so easy for you! You're so stupid!" He wouldn't accept my apology. I had thought it was good business. I thought I succeeded in solving the problem, maintaining good relations while saving his reputation all within minutes. I was wrong. Alen was now so upset he shouted at me to leave and suggested I sleep with this friend of mine while I was so willing to offer things for free anyway. "Obviously you already have! How else would a guy just hand over that much money to you!" He stormed out of his office as I stood, alone, staring after him as though he would magically reappear and make everything ok. He wouldn't. He never did, never would. I turned and saw Mia, head still down, seated quietly and doing her best to stay focused on her scribbles. She held her own. Her book open, but her pen made no movement. She simply froze and waited instruction. My perfect little angel, always knowing how to stay below the radar. Always knowing how to avoid adding to troubles, to this life I was faulted for.

Driving through a windy, winter blizzard, Mia and I picked Kris up and drove to Bowden to get the cheque. This took just over two hours due to poor road conditions. I was stressed as I now only had another hour left before the bank would close. I was stressed because this was all now worthless. I ruined my good deed with my offer for compensation. I ruined it. I went on to pick up the cheque, I wouldn't even be able to stay a bit to thank my friend for his help. I would have to grab the money and run. I was so uncomfortable now knowing that Alen thought this friend and I had some sort of relationship other than pure. He was such a good man. I was so sorry for him, knowing Alen thought this of him. Of us. I was so embarrassed.

I quickly thanked him and explained my rush, then raced to the bank before it closed and deposited the funds into the business account. I had no access to this account, never would, but knew the number so I would always be allowed to make deposits, but never anything beyond that. Alen had explained this when the account had been opened. I wasn't to be trusted and I had nothing to do with his company, I was only a wife. I was only to know what he wanted to share with me. I understood. I accepted. I was only to follow his requests, his orders. I was happy to do so. I had many other duties to complete. All duties were welcome, they gave me a purpose, I was useful. As long as I was useful, my kids would have their Mom, I would have my kids.

I returned later that evening to the office and Alen sat in his office playing games on his new computer, as others worked diligently in the shop to complete service orders into the night. Alen was agitated, the stress of the day had gotten to him and he was now exhausted from the demands of owning his business. He reminded me how I would never understand this stress, this overwhelming obligation he had to ensure his family had food on the table, that every employee had food on their table. He reminded me that as just a wife, I simply would never understand what it was like for him. I had it so easy. He went on to explain the other duties that now needed to be done, that I neglected as I took so long getting back to the office. He said if I wasn't too tired from sleeping around, he would give me the list to tackle. I began tackling each task, while my kids sat close by, on the floor quietly playing. Alen, now so exhausted from the stress he had just gone through having to wait for my return to ensure I completed the financial transaction, the stress of my throwing money away, the stress that I apparently slept around, finally left to have drinks with friends. He needed a break. Much too stressful a day. I would stay to finish whatever I could, ensure the guys in the shop continued their work, then go home and return the following day to continue as I was never really finished, ever. Somehow, I was unable to ever finish this growing list of tasks. I feared I was going to lose. I needed to try harder. Do more. Stay longer. All the while, I had my kids. Thank God I had my kids. This was all that really mattered.

Kris was silent. He slept soundly by the desk I sat at for hours that night. Mia too fell asleep alongside him. How had their day been? Had this been his first day at school? Or was that yesterday? Maybe last week? I missed it after all. I missed many moments. They were with me so often but I missed so much. They had to be quiet. I needed to focus on getting work done. Ensuring Alen was stress free. Ensuring my kids were ok. Why was I so worried for them?

It went on like this for years. I developed the company website and maintained it. I worked to ensure staff were performing their duties. I played the 'bad guy' role at all times as Alen needed to be the good guy, the great guy, the guy who could do it all. I worked in multiple roles depending on what Alen needed of me on any given day. I had been the receptionist then trained them. I was involved with local and international sales and eventually managed them. I managed projects both in the shop and out of the shop. I oversaw scheduling. I aided and often had to follow up on parts orders, then many times, had to pick up parts. I often had to source and purchase special parts after hours, pleading with vendors to meet with me so I would be able to bring necessary parts to staff working through the night. I became a customer liaison and often times lied to many, reassuring them that Alen was away on a service call when in fact, he was either somewhere socializing and having a few drinks or, I really wouldn't know where he was. Perhaps buying more street drugs or vitamins as he called them. Maybe he had injected too much HGH once again and needed to let off some steam. I wouldn't know. I wouldn't ask. Somewhere along the line I learned not to ask. There were times I would try to remember but panic would begin and I'd fear another breakdown. It could be worse than the one I had before.

I helped with accounting and all legal matters, as long as they didn't apply to the ownership or shares of the company as these were off limits to me. This was none of my business, as Alen would remind me. I aided human resources and often, I was human resources. I was responsible to apply for and obtain certification with Canada Body Builders which gave Alen's company the official stamp from Canada for building new units. A lengthy process involving paperwork, applications and working closely with engineers. Alen was admired for achieving this so quickly. Obtaining funds and loans when Alen neglected to follow up on invoicing and payroll or payments were needed. Eventually, I was overseeing all invoicing and ensuring they were completed and sent out, with Alen's final approval first of course. With Alen's signature once all was complete of course. It was always to be understood that Alen had done all the work after all, that's what I needed to ensure everyone always believed. Eventually, Alen hired an office manager and I worked closely with him. Even though this manager was exceptional at his duties, I was still required to work closely with him and always ensure I took responsibility should there ever be a problem with Alen's spending. Justifying every purchase or withdrawal after the fact, as I had never deserved to understand beforehand. I was just a wife.

Housekeeping became part of my daily routine and I was to ensure everyone played their part in maintaining a safe and clean work environment, both in the office and in the shop and eventually, in the service trucks. I aided with quoting processes and eventually, created and completed all quotes. Again, with Alen's signature prior to sending them out. Eventually, I had a jpeg of Alen's signature as he didn't want to be bothered with having to be available to sign. This saved me time as well.

The list was ongoing and even though additional duties were constantly being added to my list, I always appreciated and was so grateful that I had these duties as I was still useful. I had my children. The reason for life, the reason for living. They were the most important to me and even though the ugly shot of guilt would rise within me, the awful feeling of how they would never join regular childhood sports or activities, they would never get to have playdates or trips, they would never understand what their friends at school spoke of when they were chatting about the wave pool or even simple family strolls, they were with me. They were protected. They had food, shelter and clothing. As long as we all behaved, we would be ok. I would dream that one day they would be free. Free to play. Free to roam. I had to get them to the end of high school. Somehow I had to work day and night until the years would pass, then they would be free. They would get to live their lives and be free. If I could work harder, they could be free sooner but Alen was never satisfied with my work or my efforts. The day would eventually come, high school, I would let them go. I would set them free. I would remain with Alen, forever. I would ensure all he needed would be my responsibility, not theirs. My kids would run free. I had to enjoy every moment I had with them until the day came when I could set them free.

While I continued to work through my days, my weeks, my months and years, Alen was able to travel and take vacations. He deserved them. He was exhausted most days, waiting for me to finally finish tasks, duties. He had so much stress caused by my laziness and had to use up his energy wondering if I wouldn't complete them on time. He would oftentimes have to question me when I spoke too long to one of the shop guys, he'd have to waste energy wondering if I formed inappropriate relationships. I caused him such anxiety, the need for time away and time with friends and yes, time with other ladies that knew far better than I, how to treat a man. They had time for him that I did not. I was far too busy with business, with my children, to give him the time he needed as a man, to feel appreciated and wanted. I was too slow to finish work on time to be able to spend any with him. I understood this and didn't question.

This was why he had to stay out all night, many times, never having to tell me who had comforted him each time. This was why he had to take summer bike trips to Sturgis and I would be so happy for him, he so deserved these getaways, after all, I was far too slow to complete my tasks and I couldn't expect him to suffer so long. This was why I had to cut my hair short and wear looser fitting clothes. He hated my long hair and not only did it always fall and he would be so annoyed with this, he would have to watch as men looked my way. Why would I do this to him? I was allowed to wear tighter clothing only when important clients were visiting. Several times he even suggested I wear short skirts for these visits. This, I wouldn't follow through with as I understood he was simply testing my faithfulness to him. Hide everything. Keep covered. No one would then be tempted and I wouldn't be as inviting. After leaving the office many times, late in the night with my children, I'd get home only to put my kids to bed, then fire up my laptop as Oman was now awake, UAE and Egypt were ready to work. I spent nights answering emails, confirming orders, preparing quotes and offering support in Alen's absence. He needed his break. He was out getting what he couldn't get at home, from me. He was out, unwinding from the stress of having to deal with the guys, with me. We were all too slow, too lazy. He would say I didn't even care for my own appearance, much less for him. I couldn't win.

All the while, I would explain to the guys, the ladies at work, even to those overseas, that Alen was busy ensuring work was getting done yet again, even through the night and they would have to accept my responses, my input and my involvement. I would explain that Alen had been rushed away on a service call to save the day! If I was at the office, I would say Alen was stuck at home on his laptop, working diligently at quotes for overseas! This is what kept the company so successful after all, Alen's dedication. All lies. Lies that I had to convince others were truths. Most days, I convinced even myself they were truths. Eventually, I developed solid relations even globally while maintaining Alen's reputation, ensuring everyone believed he was involved with all decisions and communications. I even planted seeds that grew admiration others had for Alen, and his father. Eventually, no one would even ask for Alen or Chris and simply asked for me. Afterall, Alen was far too busy running the company and Chris, well, he was simply too important to be bothered.

Yes. Kreso, or Chris as everyone called him, joined Alen shortly after the company began and after I had won his lawsuit against a large oil company, my second win for the Trio. I couldn't recall Alen's lawsuit well but I definitely remembered Chris's. I enjoyed this case and had such a passion for law I nearly considered pursuing it as a career. Thank goodness Alen reminded me that I would have to serve coffee to Lawyers and be their pee on way before I would ever reach the Bar. I quickly lost that ambition and was perfectly happy to know I could be a Lawyer, if I ever wanted to be. I was privileged to take Chris's case and was successful.

With this joining of forces between father and son, I had even more responsibilities. To ensure both father and son had the admiration and respect from all, from everyone. Both father and son were an incredible team, a great duo and without them, the company would be nothing. In exchange for my efforts, both Alen and his father had time to smile, to joke around, to play games with staff and visitors, to ensure everyone saw just how easy running the business came to them. They were naturals. I had peace from their constant concern for my mental health and ability to care for my children. Yes. They were carefree most of the time and I was happy to ensure this continued, that it was a constant. They had the time to sit and chat, to entertain, to go out for drinks or to even stay in for drinks. If they weren't able to do all of these things, I was to blame and somehow, some way, my peace was gone. I would soon realize I must have been too slow or too lazy. They would say that maybe they didn't need me after all. I knew what would happen if I wasn't needed. It wasn't something I could explain, I had no idea how I knew, I just knew. I just, simply, knew.

These were the times I worked the hardest and forgot any feeling of stomach pain, sleepiness or guilt for my kids. I focused on my missions and remained steadfast to them. I never heard Alen or Chris tell me I did a good job. I was never thanked. I was never good enough or fast enough. This never bothered me although at times, I noticed it bothered others. All I truly needed to know, was said without words. If they were silent and content, I was doing what was required of me. If they said they thought I wasn't needed, I wasn't being useful, this was life threatening to me. It would create a sense of doom. An awful pounding in my chest would overcome me and I would have a hard time breathing. I would then work harder. When I worked harder, longer and with more passion, the pounding in my chest went away. I was able to breathe. They would become silent again. This didn't have to make sense, not to me. I welcomed the relief and felt safe again. I was safe again regardless of not knowing what triggered such panic. Such fear. It went away each time I worked harder, longer and with more ambition. That's all that mattered.

This was why it was such a great thing I was never put on payroll. I never received a paycheck. I never earned a wage. Ever. Not by choice, but I understood. I would have been an even bigger burden than I already was had they added me to this debt they owed the world every two weeks. Besides, I really wasn't working to their expectations and didn't have a title, a position or a steady office space to work from. I simply had to stay busy, keep working. Alen had already suffered so much as each payroll that passed, he would be with Chris complaining about how worthless the staff had been and these people didn't deserve such wages. Such freeloaders. Afterall, without father and son, there would be no company. These people who worked for them, enjoyed the frequent barbecues, the games, the wages. They all used Alen and his father and even they didn't deserve the wages they were given so graciously by the father and son duo. This is what they both complained about constantly, behind closed doors of course.

These freeloaders were only using them for their own enjoyment, therefore, Alen and Chris were forever victims of what others could get from them. Yes, this was how it was to them, behind closed doors, while drinking their time away. Oh the misery they both felt with how much everyone had used them. Thank goodness Mara had the time to console them, to reassure them that they were heroes to all and everyone would one day see just how much both Alen and Chris had done for them! She would make them drink after drink to console their woes, crown royal in each mix. She was always so supportive, so reassuring, so angry with the world for always being against her husband and son and taking advantage of them. *"Do they not know how important and incredibly brilliant you both are?!"* She would shout. Of Course not, everyone was always only out to use them. This was simply the way it was.

Every so often I felt that Alen may have experienced some guilt. Maybe he saw just how hard everyone had worked to ensure the company was a success. Just how much everyone did appreciate him and his father. Every so often, Alen would insist I buy a ton of steaks, always top grade. He would remind me that I needed to get the bread that I was to cut into slices, not pre sliced, the guys all liked that one the best. He would instruct me to buy the salads, the corn and of course, reminded me not to forget the plates and utensils. I would spend the night after work on these occasions, running to the store and buying the necessities and often times, having to go to several stores as they wouldn't have all the steaks I needed in one place. Then I prepared and seasoned all the steaks, wrapping them tight. I ensured they were in the fridge even if I had to remove all of our own food to make sure they would fit. I would prepare the bread, cut, buttered and seasoned. Wrapped those up too. Kids beautifully sleeping, just a few feet away. I was happy to do it each time and each time I would wake early to make sure I had it all packed in my car, not forgetting a single item I was instructed to bring. Of course I enjoyed this, I knew as long as I did these things and didn't make mistakes, Alen, Chris and even Mara, would all get to glow and take in the praise, the glory and the appreciation of all those who attended. I looked forward to these days as even though I may have felt a hint of fatigue, I would get to have that much more time to prove I was useful. Alen and Chris would simply fire up the BBQ once everything was set out for them, and I would gain some time to catch up on the work I missed while preparing for the event.

There had been times someone took notice of my absence at one of these BBQ's and Alen would come storming into the office and demand my presence as people were beginning to question him. *No! This was never good!* I had to ensure there were never any questions, not directed to Alen that is.

My heart would pound when I heard of anyone questioning my involvement or my absence. *Please don't question. Why would they do this to me?* All I wanted was some time to catch up, to remove some of the items on my list so I could move forward, get more done! Why couldn't they see that they should ignore me? Ignore my presence? I didn't exist? They should be focusing on Alen, on Chris, on fun. I would panic. Alen was angered by these questions and in turn, I was running to put yet another fire out, while ensuring no one knew flames now consumed me.

I would run out to ensure all was well and everyone would see, I was simply 'anti social' as always or had to make a phone call or whatever excuse I could think of in the situation. They needed to see I was smiling and simply didn't care for their socializing, their unnecessary need to have fun. I was far too serious and stale for such things. So sorry for not wanting to attend. So sorry I almost missed it. So sorry I am such a bitch who hates you. So sorry I don't eat. Yes. So glad you all see how Alen is such a Saint to even be with me, as miserable and boring a person that I am. I would do my part and once I saw everyone was reset back to joy, back to not questioning, back to fun and back to focusing on Alen, I would return to my temporary office and back to work I went. Other times, I would sit and eat and socialize. I did whatever I had to. Work would always be there waiting for me.

Through the years, I developed only some friendships. Only those that Alen found might benefit him somehow. Presidents and owners of companies, various vendors and some customers. Yes, these were welcome friends to me. I appreciated them and I also appreciated the fact that Alen approved. I had very little friends otherwise. I understood I wasn't a very well-liked person and Alen would remind me to be grateful for what little friendships I had. When Alen or his parents didn't approve, I was no longer allowed certain friendships. This again, I didn't even think to question. It just was. I simply knew this was how it worked. I needed approval and I sought it, I asked for it, I would never think to act on my own. I would never think to make decisions on my own. This would be absurd. Although, when I would start to really think about things, I would know there had been times I questioned or even argued. That panic feeling would make its appearance and I would quit the train of thought.

Sometimes I felt I may have developed a friendship with an employee and would be happy. Alen would quickly remind me that those who were kind to me or made small talk with me, simply felt sorry for me. They knew I lacked social skills. Others, he would say, only showed me this respect out of respect for him. Without Alen, these people would simply hate me and never associate with me. I would quickly stop these small conversations, knowing they were fake, regardless of the joy it would bring me. No one really wanted to talk to me, they were only playing games, playing parts, everyone had a role. They were against me. How silly of me to think otherwise.

15 PART FIFTEEN
2009
A DEMON TOWERING OVER ME

The ceiling. Must be. White. Trying to focus. It's so blurry. I was on the floor. Yes. What happened? I might have tripped. Backwards. Yes backwards when he came at me. I must have.

Alen stood high above me, taller than I remembered him to be. He was a monster, a demon towering over me. Glaring down, burning through my soul. My eyes could hardly stay open as I struggled through the blur, the fog, trying to focus. Such hate. Such evil. Oh God. *Please help me.*

Veins swollen over his brow. Throbbing at his neck. Fighting to break through skin as they rushed his arms down to his giant, clenched hands. He was watching me. My eyes failed. Too much fog. *Where is he?* Open your eyes! I demanded myself to open my eyes! Blurry, foggy, open. There he is, still standing. Watching me.

Chest heaving. Slight sweat. Skin looked deep red, burned, as though a flare ignited right before his eyes. His eyes. They were so clear, almost see through with nothing behind them.

He was watching me, looking for something. Searching for my eyes. He raised his fist to hit again. Yes, again. No. Not again. He threw me first. Yes. That's how I'm here, on the floor. With both hands, he threw me back. When I raised mine to block myself. My arms were blocking my head, my face. He grabbed my wrists. Threw me back. My legs lifted. I was flying. Then it ends. I woke on the floor. How far has he thrown me? Where was I?

His clenched hand now fanned out as he raised it above his shoulder, each thick finger now spread wide. Slamming down with force. The smack sent me rolling to the wall. *Will he just say something! Please just scream at me! Shout!* The silence was too painful. Oh God. *Help me!*

"*Can you hear me now?* You awake yet, *bitch!?*" He shouted as he hit the floor dropping to his knees.

Yes! Yes! I am! I hear you! *Why can't I scream?!*

I fought to stay awake. Stay awake or he'll strike again! Show him your eyes! Open your eyes! *Turn your head dammit!* I shouted within myself, my body ignored my screams. I screamed for help, my voice failed me. I struggled and groaned and formed whatever sound I could push through my dry lips. They were so dry. Spikes of pain shot through my head as I pushed myself from the wall and rolled myself toward him. My tailbone jolted and throbbed now. It must have broken again. The pain was unbearable. I had to move! Yes! I moved! He has to see I'm awake! The pain strikes again and I wince. No! Open your eyes! *Open your fucking eyes!*

He snickered. Yes, he sees me move. He hears my sounds. Thank God!

Now crouched low, bent, knees inches from my abdomen as I lie there, still foggy. I lifted my hand to push him back but gently rested it on him instead.

I had no strength. I touched him. Where was Alen? What was this evil thing doing this to me? Where's God? I stopped praying again. *This must be why! I'm so sorry!!*

"You want more?!" He screamed. "Do you want to tell me again how you're leaving? How awful I am? Do you want to tell me again what a shitty person I am? What a shitty father I am!" He screamed every word as a Drill Sergeant to his useless recruit.

"Those useless kids of yours? You support them and **never me**! How about I show them what it feels like to **WANT TO DIE**?" My heart raced, pounded through my veins. So loud. The beat was so loud my ears deafened with every beat, breaking the sound of his voice every other second. I was trapped beneath a monster who spat threats relentlessly. Oh my God! *Hear my screams!*

"You listen to me now! Hear *every* word I'm about to say!" He snarled, coming closer as I lay motionless on the floor. "Are you listening?" He spat, demanding I acknowledge him. I always had. Always did. Always would. Acknowledge I understood. I heard. I listened. I respected. Yes. I nodded, regardless of the pain. I must have. Yes, I was listening and forced my eyes to stay open. *Stay open!* Tears soaked my skin.

"You ever threaten to leave me again," he took a breath, a break, a reset to ensure I was really hearing every word. He reached down and grabbed my shirt within his grip, scratching my skin as he lifted me closer to him. *Ignore the pain. No pain.* He demanded I hear him, look him in the eyes. I did. I had woken up. I was alert and aware and hearing his every word. He had my full attention.

"I will *kill* them. I will kill them and you will live. You will live with the guilt that it was all your fault. They'll kill *themselves* if they're smart! Either way, **they will die!**" The last three words came directly into my ear. I felt his breath, the heat sent shivers through me. A forced whisper, pauses between each, to be clear, I heard each word. "Go ahead! Leave! I dare you!" He laughed. He was now laughing. I knew this laugh. This laughter without joy, without life. "You have nowhere to hide!!" He released his grip as though letting a moldy rag fall free in disgust. I fell once again to the floor, my head now searing with pain. My back almost numb. He raised himself and stood tall, proud, still glaring at me with eyes so clear and full of hate, full of evil. He meant every word. He smiled. Satisfied I was paying attention. I understood. Lord only knew what expression I gave as I laid there motionless. He spat on me with disgust, then left.

Silence now around me. Quiet. Peace. I listened for each sound as he stormed away. The garage door slamming. Car engine revving. Gravel shooting the house as he sped from our driveway. He was gone. Thank God, he was gone.

Kris. Mia. I'm so sorry. I failed again. I believed you. I remembered only some. Pictures and clips played through my mind. Some only seconds, some almost minutes. Keys. Yes. Now I remember. The weight of the ring of keys. Your poor face. Your poor soul. Alen had whipped them at your face from across the room. Not far, maybe 5 feet? He was sitting on the couch at Mara's, you stood just by the little step. He was so angry with you for saying the things Rob told you to say. *You were just a kid.* I know you thought you were following the rules, listening to the older people. But he had you make fun of Alen. *This wasn't your fault!* But the keys I'm sure made you feel that it was. Made you understand to never do it again. Alen was so angry he whipped them directly at your head. They hit your face, your cheek, and left wounds. Kreso and Mara were there. They said nothing. They did nothing. Other than offer Alen a drink after he stopped yelling at you. *Oh my God why can't I remember what followed?!*

The whip of his belt. You were so small. I remembered bits. I'm trying. Trying so hard to remember it all. The pain. Your pain. Then Kris, you were dragged by the collar of that blue jacket. Blue jacket. Your small body being smacked into the wall. Dragged again then crashing up against the couch. Dragged again and again. Thrown around like an old, dirty blanket needing to be whipped of dust and dirt. Blue jacket. You had that jacket in grade one. I think it was grade one.

Mia, you just wanted him to see you. To hear you. He was awful. *You have to know you're innocent.* You're none of those awful words he shouts at you! Oh how I wish you would somehow not hear him. Not hear those words. Not feel the pain of the things he says.

But you're *alive*. You'll both understand. I'm protecting you. You don't know it but I'm trying. I'm so sorry.

My eyes allowed for my escape and I drifted away. Beautiful sleep. Just sleep. It would take me away. Far away. Nothing to worry about when I'm far away from here.

This is the home Mara and Kreso stay in, for free, without my consent ever.
Look above in the clouds. Do you see it?
I took this photo myself when looking up to pray, once again, asking for answers.

16 PART SIXTEEN
2019
TEN YEARS GONE BY. BROKEN ROAD TO FREEDOM.

The Countdown to July 2019.

Ten years since I was on the floor looking at the ceiling in our home in Conrich just outside Calgary. Ten years since I cried, saying sorry to my children within my thoughts as words couldn't be spoken. Ten years since Alen's parents forced me to fire my own brother, giving me no other choice. Kreso threatened to not only bankrupt him, but to never repay his investment should I not fire him and ensure it appeared to be entirely my decision. *Entirely.* I could let no one, absolutely no one know it wasn't my own decision. I would learn years later that Alen was in fact a part of this ploy as well. He knew all along. Yet they tested me, for years, to see how committed and trustworthy I truly was. I had proven time and again that I was completely under their control. I would do and say anything I was instructed to, truly believing I was saving lives.

Nine years since Alen dealt with two of his own friends in order to isolate them from me and put an end to their questioning.

Alen drugged his friend Alex under the guise that it was some random patron in a Red Deer Pub who must have done the deed. No, Alex began noticing Alen's disrespectful behavior toward me. No one should ever question Alen but Alex started to do just that. No one should ever get close to me but Alex was doing this as well. Although I thought Alen didn't know that I was beginning to trust Alex, I soon realized he knew too well. Alex was gaining my trust which was not an easy mission.

To teach me a lesson in keeping to myself and never disobeying, Alen drugged Alex proving to me just how far he would go and how he could get away with whatever he chose to do. He proved to me that he would hurt anyone that interfered with this life he created. He proved to me that those who tried to gain my trust would suffer and this was only a small example as it would only get worse. That night, Alen called me first. I was the only call he intended to make. He said with a slight snarl and half giggle, that Alex had been a victim of a random drugging and was crying out for help. He was crying out for my sister Marija to help him and I could hear Alex begging Alen to call for help. He was terrified and I remembered feeling this way back in 2005 when my body and mind were shutting down and only Alen could save me, yet it was Alen and his parents who had drugged me. All the while, Alex lay waiting beside Alen as he spoke to me on the phone, describing Alex's misery and simply wanting me to feel the danger and his ability to refuse Alex any help or rescue. He could simply leave him helpless or drug him even more. No one would ever think it to be Alen and he could simply, as always, place the blame on others. I needed to be aware that he held the power and could use it at any time, without guilt or fear. I needed to understand that should I continue to trust Alex, there would be no phone call or rescue to save him.

I was Terrified. Alen asked me what he should do next and I fully understood his question. This was my lesson to be learned yet Alex was the one who had to pay the price. I begged Alen to call an ambulance, but he refused. I then begged him to call Marija because I could hear Alex's cries. With my promise to obey and never, ever trust anyone again, Alen called Marija and allowed Alex to talk with her. Soon after this, the ambulance was finally called and Alex was taken to the hospital. I never spoke with Alex again other than short, work related sentences. I stayed away from him as much as I could, which was extremely difficult as we still worked together within Alen's company. I was always worried that even the most innocent discussion I had with him would send Alen on to a deadly path. I did my best to avoid many people moving forward. Always.

Then, Alen stole over $30k from Rick, a longtime friend. Rick was told to bank many hours he worked machining for Alen and the company. He was promised by Alen, that Alen would pay him in full when Rick requested to be paid. Alen of course refused to pay Rick his money when the time came. Rick wanted to begin to rebuild his life after losing his wife unexpectedly and asked Alen for his payment so he could move forward. Alen owed Rick just over $30,000.00 and had also promised him shares of the company.

Rick told others that he would tell me the truth and refused to allow Alen to intimidate him. I heard from others of how Rick was coming to tell me of things Alen had hidden or tried to hide from me for so many years. Rick's Mom also put the word out that the life Alen and I portrayed was in fact a lie and people should know the truth. People, including me.

Alen, of course, had other plans and would silence Rick and his family. He told everyone that Rick was lying, completely unstable and not to be trusted and then obtained a restraining order on this longtime friend of his. Alen wanted to ensure Rick understood the authorities would sooner believe Alen's word, a successful businessman, over Rick's word at any given time. Alen walked around wearing a bulletproof vest hidden underneath his shirt and jacket for weeks following this event. In order to stop any further destruction, I convinced Alen and his parents that I would never, *ever* believe a word Rick or his Mom may ever say to me. That no matter what they could or would ever say, I would never believe them.

Alen set out to ensure no one would ever tell me truths or get close enough for me to trust. Awful. Horrible. Inexcusable what he had done to others in order to save only himself and the life he so wanted and needed to live. This life full of drugs, money, power, women, servants. **Both** friends were threatening to tell me truths. Both friends were punished. Soon after these friends were 'dealt with', one was drugged and the second robbed then shunned, Alen moved on to another 'friend' who was far more obedient and loyal than these old friends had been. To this very day, he has this man's full loyalty and blind obedience. An obedience that Alen even tested by convincing this friend to leave his wife and soon after that, his girlfriend. Alen did not want this new, loyal friend to ever have anyone else in his life he would have to be loyal to other than him. There was no room for this. Alen learned this through time and would not allow for any instability in the loyalty of a friend he chose moving forward. This friend needed to only have loyalty towards Alen, no one else.

Eight years since winning yet another legal wish for the Trio and hurting so many in the process. The Norwegians, led by one of the Trio's close family friends, came to invest and work together with the Trio to ensure the company grew and became even stronger, offering even more to the industry than ever before. The Norwegians were the only group to ever put me on payroll at the company. They did it, when no one else ever would. This group had every intention of fulfilling their agreement and continue to build the company.

Alen and his parents wanted to make their money and walk away, never to have to work again. Alen and his parents never had any intention to grow the company with this group or to work with them. They would not be viewed as beneath anyone, no matter what. This wasn't what the original plan had been, and the Norwegians fought for themselves and were angered with the Trio for changing their intentions, their goals and their promises. Unfortunately, Alen and his parents had me fight for them. Although Alen didn't get his millions, he did get more than he ever deserved and walked away from his commitments. He got much more than he ever deserved and instead of being sued himself by the Norwegians, he won against them and walked away, never having to lift a finger in doing so. He ordered me to complete it all. Abandoning not only his commitments to them, but to all of his staff and clients as well. I made this happen as I had made many things happen when ordered by the three. I was sorry, but would not be able to disobey and prayed I would one day be able to forgive myself, once again, for so many wrongful actions I played a role in. Always, I played the only traceable role. Everything would be traced back to me and in the end, the Trio constantly reminded me of this fact. I couldn't win. I couldn't escape.

I then spent even more time in isolation and seclusion because I simply wanted to. It was no longer an order from Alen, it was a wish of my own. I wanted to be alone. I didn't want to be with others, to face them, to continue to lie to them. To hurt or destroy them. To place them in danger. To have them exposed to any form of attack by the three. I wanted to stay away from everyone. I didn't want any more people hurt. Betrayed. Lied to.

Seven years since I was forced to open another company, this time, on my own. No one to help me as Alen had to be safe guarded due to his non-compete. Kreso and Alen, with Mara always their ever-supporting cheerleader, insisted I open another manufacturing and service company and run it. They needed more money and I was to get it for them. I was forced to begin another journey to take me into the trapped life with the Trio. No choice was ever given. I was instructed on what needed to be done and I did it. Open a business and run it. On my own. I did it. I hated it. I hated the fact that I was forced to do this. I continued my lie, my instructed life and performed as always to expectations. Never allowing anyone to see or sense that I hated it, rather, everyone had to believe it was my life and love. It was my wish. I was running an oilfield manufacturing and service company all on my own and enjoyed every minute of it. Yes, I made this happen and no one was to even question whether it was true or not. Ever. I safeguarded the Trio and ensured they had money to continue to spend on their lifestyle and whims. Again, I was earning the money that they were spending, endlessly. Yes, I made millions and they spent it.

Most often during this time, my kids and I were living in emotional trauma with only intermittent physical abuse. The physical abuse had decreased but never fully stopped.

Six years since I began the process of transferring my business to another local company in order to ensure my employees were cared for and didn't suffer due to 'my choices'. Our house in Conrich, just outside of Calgary, had been placed up for sale and we began preparations for a move without my consent, input or will, but with my full cooperation as was always required. Everything to do with the sale was again, my duty. Everything. I then had to ensure Mara and Kreso's home was for sale as well and again, all was on my shoulders to ensure success in achieving their goals. Not mine. Not my children's. Ever.

Five years since I began a journey that took me even further into isolation and exhaustion, slavery and deprivation. Owning the businesses and working together was eventually not enough. The Trio decided we were to live together as one. Alen, Chris and Mara decided we would move in together, kids and I had no choice. We were never asked or involved with any decision making. This was always the Trio, the three, their authority and right.

We listened as the Trio told others their story of how a family meeting was held, asking us our wishes. A meeting to ensure my kids and I were totally on board and wished the same as they had, to live together, happily ever after. Never happened. Never would. We moved to a quarter section south of Sundre with two homes on the property that Alen and I purchased. Again, as I had never spent, most of the funds were technically my hard work and dedication that purchased the property and many assets. This would never be known to others. This was simply how it was and would be.

My kids and I did almost all of the packing and unpacking. We followed the story lines, played our parts and never admitted the truth. Never. Simply couldn't. Again, everyone thought us to be an even more perfect family after this move, even more perfect than ever before. So united. So together. So strong. So **perfect**.

Four years since the RCMP were called out to the farm. Stories succeeded, RCMP left, neighbours left. We were once again 'safe'. Details would be part of a second book as while writing this first, the trial has yet to have taken place.

Three years since the RCMP made yet another visit to our farm. Details would be a part of a second book as while writing this first, again, the trial has yet to have taken place. This would be the year that triggered even worse events than ever before. It would be one that I would forever regret not telling the RCMP the truth at this point, at the three-year countdown, of what *really* happened on this day. Instead, I lied. I stayed quiet. I refused to betray Alen and kept him safe, as always. Had I told the truth then, my kids would have been **safe**. Instead, they were put through even more trauma and hell that unfortunately was severe. It should never have happened. I should have spoken the truth and finally saved them. They wanted to speak the truth but wouldn't, to protect me. Not themselves, but me. How I would ever forgive myself for this would remain an impossible thought and quite honestly, may never actually happen. *How would I ever forgive myself? I would never deserve my forgiveness.* This, I truly believed.

Two years since suffering what I now know to be too much trauma for my mind to accept and finally realize just how severe my life had become, and always was. Just how severe my children had lived while I blindly and obediently forced them to stay and continue to live the insanity. I still battled myself and would return to hiding the truth in some sort of compartment within my mind. I still fell into times when I couldn't see the truth but at least the clarity began. Intermittent as it was, I began having clarity. Several incidents happened throughout the year. Several. We should never have stayed. I was so wrong. I was *so very wrong.*

One year since I *fought* myself, *screamed* at myself, *pleaded* with myself to figure out a way to free my kids! It was only *getting worse!* Just like every year before! Each year that passed, it was only getting worse. I still believed we would be saved from death because I followed the rules, played the game, told the stories, isolated everyone and as long as I stayed, we'd escape death. I *still believed* my kids were safer at the farm than away. There would come a day when I wouldn't be able to understand this thought pattern and as I would write these words, I would know I believed we were safer staying. As I believed it for years. As I believed it when guns were pointed directly at us. As I believed when I'd be knocked unconscious. As I believed when my heart would race as I watched him torture my kids. He convinced me it would be worse. He convinced me there was no escape. I believed it no matter what. I was convinced. I know now, I was so very wrong.

Just over 7 months since fleeing for the very last time. It's never too late. *Never say never.* There have been **many** who would not reach this last time and never return to their abuser. It was too late for so many. I am one of the fortunate ones who can say, it's never too late while knowing, it easily could have been too late.

> Alen >
>
> Mon, Dec 24, 9:44 PM
>
> Just goes to prove that it's 3 against 1. Fuck to guys
>
> Don't be staying at a hotel either, not on my dime

17 PART SEVENTEEN
MY KIDS AND I FLED OUR LIVES IN DOMESTIC VIOLENCE, ABUSE AND CONTROL FOR THE VERY LAST TIME ON DECEMBER 24, 2018. CHRISTMAS EVE.

I can't even begin to tell you all the places my kids and I have stayed. No really, it's not a figure of speech, I *really* can't tell you. Life after fleeing isn't a life one can easily describe. The state of mind of the abuser is terrifying and anyone who believes those who flee are safe once they've left, really don't know the mind of an abuser or the life of a victim. They don't understand the mental state of either. It isn't a life of freedom imagined when hearing, *"why didn't you just leave?"*. I often wonder what it is that those who haven't lived in abuse, lived the life of domestic violence think of when they say, *"why didn't you just leave?"* or *"thank God you're now free!"*

Free. Thinking back, there was nothing free about fleeing, escaping, running, leaving, absconding. There was no sense of freedom. Not emotionally, financially or physically. I was not free. I was thrown into a whirlwind, a tornado of emotion and had nowhere to go. I was terrified. I was confused. I was questioning everything, including if I made the wrong decision. All I had was a car and my children. Yes, in the grand scheme of things this is all I would ever need. But in reality, in life, we needed food, clothing, gas, shelter, hygiene, school and so much more. I needed to undo years of damage to my ability to think clearly. Think for myself. Think. Terror maybe, but not freedom. No, it would take a long time to understand the term 'free'. The word itself was foreign to me. It was a fantasy. It would haunt me for months, maybe years.

To be **free**.

The definition being the adjective:
1. not under the control or in the power of another; able to act or be done as one wishes.
2. not or no longer confined or imprisoned.

The definition being the adverb:
1. without cost or payment

The definition being a verb:
1. release from captivity, confinement, or slavery

As defined in the Merriam-Webster, the meaning of **freedom**:
1. the quality or state of being free: such as
    a. the absence of necessity, coercion, or constraint in choice or action.
    b. liberation from slavery or restraint or from the power of another: independence.
    c. the quality or state of being exempt or released usually from something onerous.

Writing this, nearly 8 months since fleeing for freedom, I am not free but I am safer than I have been in years. My kids are *safer* than they have ever been, ever. But they are not free. Not yet. We are not just alive anymore, we are living. With what little we have, we are living and have absolutely no regrets of finally leaving that horrible life and the monster who calls himself a husband and a father. The evil of two others who have never, ever earned the right to be called grandparents, or even parents.

We are not free, but we are living. Finally.

I've tried to compare it to those having to flee as their homes are burning or flooding. This I believe is a trauma survived by many, but as I tried to compare them to myself, my life, I found little comfort or reassurance. A fire or flood would be like a tornado or rocket. Not human. There's a fear I brought with me as I fled knowing exactly who I was running from and what he was capable of doing, anywhere, any time. Knowing he had some so loyal to him, so loyal they would do anything he asked and would even alert him of our whereabouts given the chance they saw us, or even worse, I refused to imagine the possibilities.

It would be as though regardless of how far one travelled to escape a flood, the wall of water follows them to no end and could swallow them in their sleep even as they seek safety high above on a mountain top. An immense wall of water chasing them and sensing where they were at any given time, with clouds above watching their every move and sending messages to the waters below, keeping it always aware of their position and just waiting for its moment to drown them for good. It's like the flood wasn't satisfied with destroying their home, their property and was furious they escaped with their lives. Wherever they hide, they would have to run and hide again as they hear the rush of water closing in. No, I couldn't imagine the comparison. Especially when my property, both my homes on the farm, my pets and livestock were still as they were. Nothing tore them down. Nothing destroyed their foundation. No disaster made everything disappear at once. My bed is still slept in. My photo albums still left on shelves. My everything, still as it was and I would never see any of it again. My kids and I never did own much, but we had suddenly been left with nothing.

I knew Alen's weapons were still as they were and I knew his night vision was Gen 3. I knew if we stayed in lit areas, always, he couldn't use the Gen 3 as it would damage it and ruin its function. Streetlights and parking lot lights were a must, I knew to stay within lit areas at all times. I knew that being so visible in the night with lights surrounding us made us visible as well, but there was a certain bigger danger if we were left in darkness. With light came public and stores and stations. More places to run and hide.

I knew his weapons could shoot well over 2km with precision and he had perfected his aim, his accuracy, regardless of weather or terrain. I knew he had specially made muzzles. I knew he worked on zero flare bullets with his closest friend in the privacy of our shop. I knew too much. I was never supposed to leave. I was never supposed to be able to stay away longer than a night. This was his comfort zone. His security. He knew I wouldn't dare. He just knew. He would never have to worry about me. I was controlled. I was his.

I knew he had trained for years to defend or attack an entire police force or Muslim ambush, much less me. I knew all of it far too well. He knew I would return as I was trained to return to defend him, to stand with him for the day to come when we needed to defend our home against some sort of enemy we would never really know or understand. We only knew the day was coming. He knew that my return would ensure the return of my children. They would never leave me alone with him, with his parents. They knew that had I returned without them, I would no longer exist. Even though my children wanted and desperately pleaded with me to leave with them for years, they would always return, with me, to protect me.

We were trained to stay under the radar and leave no trace. We were trained to escape hostage situations and had to practice years ago how to unbind ourselves from duct tape wrapped tightly around our wrists and watch for tails as we drove. Always aware of our surroundings. Someone was always ready to attack. Someone was always watching. Never use our real names. Never disclose too much. Never question. Never leave.

Mia's training, I would one day realize, was taken to a sick level. She was put in choke holds on a regular basis, by Alen, often leaving her breathless and far too close to death. Alen enjoyed this and *I believed* there was nothing I could do to help her. Kris was never home for these routine practices Alen had with Mia. Alen fully understood he had to control himself much more as Kris grew older. Alen wouldn't attack Mia in front of Kris.

It would be me, watching in silence as Mia lost breath, pleaded for air with pain in her eyes, staring at me as Alen laughed, squeezing her neck within his elbow, between forearm and bicep. If I made a sound he would squeeze harder. We were never to show panic. Never show fear. Never scream for help. The enemy would hear and know our location. We were in constant training for an attack, not by Alen, but by everyone and anyone who was against us. The entire time, years of training, the only one who was actually against us, was Alen. Preparing us for our deaths. Our quiet deaths. In truth, the enemy was Alen and he would kill her. If I screamed, she would die. If I called for help, it would be worse, torture followed by death. He had made these clear to me over the years. They were part of my every thought. Never would I forget what he said he would do. This was our daily life within our own home, in our own kitchen, where others would visit and see such wealth and happiness. Where others would stand and shower us with praise and appreciation for how we had a wonderful home, beautiful furnishings and the most serene views. Yes, peaceful beauty to most. A torture chamber for us.

As we drove further into the night, my thoughts were scattered and my heart raced. *Where do I go? What do I do? Where do I hide? Can he track my car?* I didn't think so, the trackers I had to buy for him just arrived. *Maybe he didn't have time to slip one in my car?* Oh I hoped not! *Can he track our phones?* No, we knew to safeguard ourselves from this! Thank God! I'll drive as far as I can and hopefully my kids will sleep, I thought. But I'm exhausted. I'm terrified. *Should I be driving?* Yes! The driver is always targeted first. Always. Tires can be hit and I had more experience, I could possibly control the vehicle should it be hit. But then again, Kris knew better. He was far more experienced in defensive driving and control of a vehicle. I couldn't do it though. I couldn't let him drive. I prayed I could control everything if shots were fired.

Who will feed our dogs? Oh God! Alen had already brutally killed two to ensure we followed his rules! We broke his rules this past year and he was realizing he was losing his control. We suffered the consequences, our pups suffered so much more. *What would he do now? What have I done?* No one will feed the animals! The cows! *Where do I go?* It's too late! My kids aren't even kids any more! They're bigger than me! *What's the point of running anymore??*

This was most likely the twentieth time we fled. Whether I knew it or not, that meant, it was also most likely the twentieth time I would go back. Whether I was aware of it or not, my mind had already begun to process how in the world to return safely. I would have to wait until he text his messages and see when he had enough time to calm down and begin convincing me he was sorry or to drown me in guilt. It would depend on his mood and his tactic of choice. He was never predictable in these ways which kept me always thinking, analyzing and trying to read situations. My mind was always overcome with assessments, analytical processes, and so forth.

Guilt would most likely be the better option. I had plenty of it and freely gave it away every day. This would take until at least the morning. Yes, I knew he would be too angry at first. He would be far too angry. Once he realized we were really gone, we hadn't returned through the night, he would cool off and start to text how he was wrong, or that he was sorry, or how I had mistreated him or disrespected him, or any number of ways to guilt me. He might text that he was hurt by something we had done and instead of talking it through, he was angry but this was just what men were taught and it wasn't his fault. There were various versions of his role as victim, whether we had created it or society was to blame or his parents were at fault, he would explain how he was simply the victim and I wasn't compassionate, I wasn't supportive, I wasn't being a wife. Then I would go back and start again. Try harder. Be quieter. The cycle would begin again with added energy, the more reason for him to teach us regret and he would translate this to teaching us 'respect'.

My kids began the process of fleeing earlier this very day, many hours before the actual time came when I joined their mission to run. Had I listened to them, I could have avoided the terror that finally sent me racing from our shop to the house to get them and speed away. Had I listened to them I would have been safer, sooner. They would have been safer, sooner. They begged me to go with them many hours before. They told me that whether I was ready or not, they would be leaving this day, even without me. They tried. They really tried. They knew there was no escaping a fatal night other than running away, hiding and never returning. They knew. I <u>still</u> stayed. I <u>still</u> asked them to wait. I <u>still</u> didn't understand what they truly saw, what they meant, what they explained. I was trained to ignore them and block out their pleas. Yes, I was trained well. I was one of Alen's best soldiers while being just the wife. Just Lucy.

When it was nearly too late, *I RAN!* I ran faster than I had ever ran before! I ran faster than when a rocket was targeting me directly, without sound, knowing it was heading right for me! A rocket would have been better. Easier to understand. Simple. A rocket was danger on a global level. Basic human instinct allowed everyone of all races, sexes, religions and ages, to understand to run. A rocket didn't know me. A rocket wasn't my husband, father to my children or childhood friend. I never feared running from a rocket. It was simply an instinct to run. *No one would ever feel guilty for trying to escape a rocket.* This would be absurd. I could have a chance to escape a rocket and would focus on my run and simply seek shelter. So much easier than this. So much easier.

Running from a man I thought I knew. Running from a man who would sooner kill his wife and children than to release his control of them. He was losing his life those around him envied. He was losing his control. He was losing his workforce. His army. His crew. He was losing everything that ever meant anything to him, his presentation of a perfect life, being the perfect man, a perfect husband and of course, a perfect father. His wife and children were only a means to maintain his true love, himself and his false world he worked so hard to create. I had escaped rockets. Rockets were easier. They could never scare me as Alen could, as Mara and Kreso could. That's what I knew this night. I was trained well. I never questioned why. I never questioned them. I never spoke of it.

As I drove further from our farm, my kids reassured me we were doing the right thing. We had no choice. We weren't to blame. We couldn't return, not this time. The three leaders, Alen, Kreso and Mara had been trying to kill us for some time already. We knew all too well that if the three leaders ever truly believed they lost control of us, our deaths would have to look as though we either died of some sort of unknown ingestion (never to be traced back to them), suicide or something I may never have been aware of. They knew what they were doing. They knew and had a plan, always prepared. They poisoned us. Each of us. There was nothing they wouldn't do to keep their false world, real.

My kids reminded me of how violently Mia had been vomiting several times in just the past month. How we would do our best not to eat Mara's food and sneak food at home without them knowing or, I would sweet talk Mara into allowing me to cook and we would watch that she didn't go near the food I made. Alen would get so angry if we didn't eat at Mara's. We knew, we knew that the food was somehow making us very sick. Our stomachs were always nauseated afterward. We were dizzy. Often wanting to sleep. When Alen was away he would call me when my kids and I wouldn't eat at Mara's. He knew. He would scold me. He would yell at me. He would threaten me. He would insist we had to join his parents for mealtimes and never miss. Before Christmas break, Kris hadn't had a decent meal in three weeks. He would rather starve to death than to continue being poisoned by his grandmother. This was our reality. This was our life.

The past month, Alen came home from being away at work and never were we to miss supper time at his parent's house. Eat. Mia handled whatever it was the worst. Migraines and vomiting. She was violently ill. I wasn't allowed to take her to the hospital. Alen insisted she was fine. He was calm. He had no concern for her at all. Without saying it, I understood he knew what was happening to her. He was far too confident and relaxed. Just as he had been in 2005 during my breakdown. He knew she would be okay. He would instruct her to force herself to vomit then sit in the shower under cold water. He insisted she would be fine. He said she had eaten too much garlic.

Yes. My kids were reminding me of reality. They told me the ugly truths and refused to hear my excuses. They were never going back and the Trio should be held accountable for their cruel, abusive and unimaginable actions. My kids were done allowing me to continue to put them in danger. They would never go back. Not even for me.

They reminded me of how much worse the past months had become as the three of us were speaking out. Kris the most, even though he had done so for years. He suffered the most but he refused to be quiet any longer, at all. He was done playing the Trio game and would no longer care to protect us, he knew this was useless. His whole life he had jumped in to be beat the most in order to protect Mia and I from Alen's assaults. His whole life he accepted he was always the villain in Alen's eyes and allowed Alen to release his attacks on him. He was ready to fight, at all costs.

Mia suffered too much as well. Her scars were physically emotional. The whip marks that had many times covered her body would disappear. One day it would be easy to explain how she had overcome the pain and knew it was not her fault. She began to fight back. Yes, this angered the Trio and the past month had been torture on us. The Trio were frustrated. They began their tactics to regain control to an extreme level. They needed to regain control or else, my kids and I, would be useless to them.

My kids spoke with ease and relief. No longer were their tones hushed trying to whisper to me. They could speak freely. They offered to drive but I insisted I was ok and really needed to be the one driving. Now I needed some sort of control as I felt it was the only thing in my entire life at that moment that I could control. A car. But it was at least something. I could focus on the road.
They asked to go to the police, the RCMP. They asked me if I would finally agree to tell the truth. To finally have Alen and his parents answer for their actions, their abuse. They needed to be held accountable. They needed to be told this was evil, wrong. Within my thoughts I screamed. *Oh Lord No! Of course not! Wasn't it good enough that I agreed to leave with them?* This was truly what I believed. *It was good enough.* We were safe enough for now. No one else needed to get hurt. If anyone else knew, they were going to be in danger. I had seen it many times before. No. I could only worry about the three of us. Adding more would be too difficult. No one would understand. Afterall, how in the world would I be able to explain how dangerous this was? I would have to write a book. There was no time to try and explain. We had to remain in silent hiding. It was safer for everyone, including the public.

Our escape to the Rocky Mountains.

18 PART EIGHTEEN
THE MOUNTAINS PROTECTED US

The night was dark. No moonlight. Snow covered the fields and trees surrounding us yet I could barely see the white. So dark. No stars. No moon. It was so very dark. So cold. I had very little money. We only grabbed a couple of pillows and toothbrushes when we ran. We only had a few clothing items when we ran. When we raced out the door. When we sped away. We only had minutes to run away from him, maybe seconds. Maybe more. He might still be in the shop confident we were quietly waiting for our destiny. Maybe he was taking his time knowing I would never think to abandon him. To run. Not now. Not when it was time to end it all. I couldn't begin to guess the situation but knew we had to speed away to safety. *He was still in the shop about 100 feet away? Maybe more?* Maybe not. I escaped the shop and ran for my life.

I ran to the house and yelled to my kids, "If you guys are serious about leaving, *we have to go now!!*" And we left. Don't look back. Don't turn around. Not until you're on a main road. Just drive! Just press the gas and drive! Lock the doors! Heads down as we sped down our driveway in case the gun is pointing, aiming. Heads down! Just in case. His pistol was in the shop. His hand gun. We knew it very well. He always had it there, in the shop, in his toolbox, left bank of drawers. He was reaching for it when I last saw him. *Heads down!*

Reaching the main road, highway 22. I focused on the road as tears streamed down my cheeks. I made no sound. It was dark. My kids were happy and they couldn't see me crying. Please don't see my tears. We drove, kept driving and were now 100 km from danger. The sense of him disappeared. His energy couldn't be felt.

Rear view mirror checks every 300 meters followed by left side view, right side view, look at the road. Repeat. Always. Never stop the checks. This was easy as I'd been trained by Alen to do these checks. I had done them for years. Part of our preparation for the inevitable attack from an unknown enemy. He said someone was always ready to hurt us. Even the police could be after us at any time. Always be aware. When we escaped from Alen and his parents, I would take these measures that were intended for daily awareness against the general public, who Alen always said were out to get us, and would use them to protect us from Alen. All clear. He should be texting soon then. He hasn't followed and sent no one to follow. No sign of police. His text will be coming soon. So far, we were in the clear.

We left at **7:09pm**, Christmas Eve. This would forever be in Mia's memory. She remembers the exact time we fled.

9:44pm. First text came in from Alen, almost three hours after we fled. The sound of my phone alerting me to the incoming text sent my heart racing. This was a regular reaction to the sounds of my phone. Normally, it would send my heart racing as I was exhausted and couldn't imagine what more chores he would assign me, parts I needed to pick up, calls I'd have to make, emails I'd have to send, spreadsheets I'd have to create, rocks I had to pick, fences I had to repair and so on. During our escapes, my heart would race because I knew, always knew, his first texts would be angry. They were always angry at first. Reminding me that he was in charge and I disobeyed. He knew I would be back. He always knew. He knew I would never tell anyone or find help from anyone. He ensured I had no trust in anyone over the years. He ensured I feared telling the truth. He ensured I would fear for the safety of those I would tell. I would never trust even the police as they were always looking for a way to hurt people and protect the criminals. He proved it over the years by showing me how victims were beat or killed, raped and abandoned, yet the criminals would be free to roam. Free. Therefore, trust no one. I had no one to go to and nowhere to go.

He also proved this by having friends within the police and friends who were undercover cops. Yes, trust no one. No one would help me. Everyone believed we were the perfect family. *Perfect*. Even when I thought of telling my family, knowing they *would* believe me, I would be putting them in the same danger we lived in for years. They could be hurt, killed. They could be dragged into a mess of lies and attacks on even their characters. At least my kids and I knew survival. We were trained. Always I reasoned with myself and ensured myself there was no one to go to, nowhere to hide for long, money would run out and so would food. I would always return. He knew. I knew. No need to question it.

His message was clear. First guilt then instruction. First ensure I felt guilty, followed by ensuring I knew my rules. Simple. Guilt had become part of my being, like breathing. It was instant. He accused us of being against him, 3 against 1. This was the guilt. Then instructed me not to stay in a hotel and not spend any money. It was his. The money, everything was his. Yes, I knew this rule well and followed it for twenty years. He spent, I scrounged.

He had luxuries, I had debt. He deserved all great things, I deserved to suffer.

We kept driving through the darkness. I could breathe again and stopped my tears, my heart relaxed. Kids and I together now enjoyed the drive. They no longer spoke to themselves knowing I wasn't listening. We were on our latest adventure, our only real holidays were these nights we fled. The only time when we didn't have to fear what would happen next because Alen simply didn't know where we were, for the time being. We had no clear destination, ever. This was a safety step. This was part of our training in preparation for 'end of the world' type scenarios. We were on an open road with our only intent being to stay hidden, not be found. Don't be seen during the escape. Don't leave a trace. Never use debit or credit. If we didn't have cash, we had nothing.

I stopped only once at a gas station to fill up with the debit card that was attached to our joint account. I had no separate account. I had no hidden savings as Alen always ensured we were cash broke and in debt. Any cash would be spent by him. Always. The past 6 months he spent over $53,000 on *himself* while my kids and I were scolded for using too much toilet paper and electricity. Yes, we had to justify everything. We were using too much heat, too many lights, keep the lights off. Don't waste his money. It was meant only for him.

I stopped only once at a gas station I knew would be difficult for anyone to determine which direction I chose to drive afterward. After this, my debit card could not be used due to the fact it would be traceable and, I was never to spend money, ever, without Alen's permission. There wasn't much in the account anyway. Never was. After this, I chose a direction with my kids and we drove onward. Further and further from 'home'.

We were safe in the mountains. The mountains that surrounded us as enormous shadows, hugging us from all sides. The mountains sheltered us from harm and protected us from demons. Truly a feeling of shelter and protection. Never will I have the words to describe this. All previous escapes I drove East, South or North. Never West. This was the first time I drove West. It was surreal.

The feeling it brought once we reached the mountains was indescribable. We couldn't see them but we felt them, we knew they were there. There's no denying that we felt them. All three of us felt them. A beautiful, positive energy and comfort. We were safe. That was enough for the night, to be safe.

It was winter, Christmas Eve. Not many people roamed around as we found our spot for the night. Most were busy celebrating with families and friends. The rest of us, those without celebration, roamed and found solace in the few gas stations or fast food locales still open to serve as we travelled alone in the world.

We parked in a well-lit area close to a fast food restaurant that would remain open through the night. The only one. We parked within a short distance from security cameras so they would watch us and capture us in case something were to happen during our stay. We parked in a well-lit area, bright lights shone all around us and we were visible, just as our surroundings were visible to us. Cameras, lighting, public. Three steps taken for safety. Our cell phones already set to remove location services. Doors locked. Key remained in the ignition with the engine off. Save fuel as much as possible but stay prepared to leave at once. More steps taken. Time to sleep. Kris folded himself at the back of the car, Mia sat in the back seat and I remained in the driver's seat. We agreed that should anyone get far too cold, we would turn the engine on to warm up, but never for long.

> God
> grant me
> the Serenity
> to accept the things
> I cannot change,
> the Courage
> To change the things
> I can,
> And the Wisdom
> To know the difference.

19 PART NINETEEN
COURAGE TO CHANGE THE THINGS I CAN

Waking on Christmas Day to our giant protectors, the snowcapped Rocky Mountains, we felt calm and reassured we hadn't dreamt of the escape and were still safeguarded and hidden. A McDonald's provided us with a place to brush our teeth and grab a cheap bite to eat. I, of course, chose to skip breakfast but coffee was a welcome treat. The night was cold, and we started the engine only twice to keep from freezing. I smiled as I watched my kids happier than I had seen them, well, since the last time we fled. Today though they seemed even happier still, as they knew, this was their final run. I wished I could be so sure.

By 11:30am Alen sent his text per tradition. His tactics would now begin. This process was simply an exchange of texts between him and I. We would text back and forth and before evening, I would be back at home, kids so loyal at my side. Guilt. His text was no longer angry, he was now beginning the guilt process. His dream home, his dream farm, his dream was now ending as he realized his wife and children had not returned through the night. He now sent words to remind me of how his dream, his world, his life was killed and we were the ones holding the knives cutting his world apart. His text explained how he would begin to sell the property and had already called a realtor. Of course, Christmas Day. Imagine that, he had already called a realtor. Of course I would never say this to him, but knew, he was always full of lies. Full of stories. Anything that needed to be said to ensure his life went back to his control, his way. He text that he would sell some items and burn the rest. He would get me money. He needed nothing, after all, it was all meaningless now. Again, he was lying. He would never, ever burn anything he owned. He cherished his possessions, more than anyone.

Yes, he knew well how to reach into my well-trained mind and pull at the strings to lure me back. Back into his world. His life. His need for control. I struggled but again, looking to my children and their smiling eyes, I put my phone down and we drove a windy dirt road to reach a mountain top and reveled in its wander. It's beauty. It's peace. This Christmas Day, my kids asked that I ignore his texts and that we give this more time. They asked if we could celebrate our first Christmas in peace, without worry, without him. They quickly distracted me with their smiles and wander of the mountainous scene they rarely, if ever, got to enjoy. A lifetime so close to the Rockies yet both kids had passed through them only a few times. Alen could wait, I thought, he could wait an hour or so until I enjoyed some time with my children. An hour turned into several as we celebrated Christmas on the run, safe for once and happy.
Christmas night was calm and quiet. I still hadn't replied to Alen. This would be the first time, ever. He expected me not to reply after receiving

his first text message the night before as I was simply being reminded and instructed. Don't disobey. Don't neglect my duty to him and don't spend his money. His money. The money I couldn't touch. The money I earned for years so he could spend it. None of it was ever mine. I understood. There's no response required to this type of message. This, I knew. This, was a given.

His second text sent on Christmas day, shortly before noon, was to be acknowledged. acknowledged. This, I knew. This, was a given. I ignored myself and the need to respond and focused on my kids and the Spirit of Christmas, not the reality of life. Not the inevitable texts that would begin to flow between Alen and myself ensuring I return home. Not the knowledge that this would soon come to an end, and we would be thrust back into our lives of horror, training, obedience, a never ending cycle that was engraved into my being. Oh how we would suffer for ruining Christmas. I could only imagine what punishment awaited. But whatever the punishment, we escaped death once again. For this I was grateful. There was nowhere else to go. Nothing else to do. The danger would reach further than I wanted to ever imagine. No, I would enjoy our time as it was soon to end. Our escape would earn us our time back in solitaire for certain with added torture. There was no other choice. I never had choices.

I was just a woman who had no education and no friends. My family wouldn't associate with me most times because I would always do and say such hurtful things, always working to safeguard them and us from the evil I knew so well. They were to never know this. No, never should they see any glimpse that I was simply protecting myself and my kids with every hurtful thing I had done, every hurtful word I said. They were to always believe it was me, who I was and who I had become. Should they ever question, as they had the first years of my marriage, this would trigger Alen and send him into a rage, a violent rage, threatening not only us but those who questioned behind closed doors. He was dangerous. He would be outraged that I slipped, that I spoke out of line, that I didn't convince them well enough of our perfect lives and they questioned him. No one should ever, ever question him. Never have even a hint of question for Alen. Never. Alen must always remain untouchable. I safeguarded him for so long, he truly believed he was in fact, untouchable and above the law, above everyone.

I was just a wife who no one would ever acknowledge and knew I had nothing to offer my household, my husband or my children. I was so indebted to Alen and his parents, for saving us all these years and keeping us sheltered and fed. Any work I may have done, any business I may have run, any legal matters I may have battled, all were nothing in comparison to what was done for me. I never questioned what was done for me. I never realized I was the one who actually provided everything, for everyone, including myself and my children.

I was just a mother. A mother who gave birth and was told I was fortunate enough to never have raised my kids the way I believed I wanted to. They would be responsible and smart because of this. They would succeed in life because I would never show them who I really was. Never. I often didn't understand the saying, never say never. Never was part of my being. Never say, never do, never be who I am or who I was. Never leave. Never fight back. Never was always meant for me. Never get sick. Never fight back. Never leave.

One day I hoped to be *just a Grandmother.*

In reality though, I was *just Lucy.*

Christmas Night my kids wanted to be alone. Kris went for a walk and Mia, although she stayed with me, we kept to ourselves to ensure the *feeling* of privacy and being alone. To be alone within our own thoughts. To have space to have our own thoughts. This was never an option at home. This was a gift on Christmas night to allow ourselves some time, some space, to be alone and enjoy some time to reflect. Hours passed and with it, we returned to each other and they gave me the news. The news that Alen had text each of them. The news that they refused to reply. The news that they insisted I understand that they were no longer a part of him. No longer a part of his life. Never really were. That from this day, they were no longer in his control.

They spoke to me as though I was a child refusing to listen to reason. In very simple terms and straight forward, they assured me that their decision was firm and there was to be no argument. No question. They would not listen to my pleas any longer. This was not up for debate. This was the way it would be. They assured me that should I decide to return on my own, they would not change their minds. They would have to accept that I accepted my fate. That I was my own person. That I was making the worst decision of my life should I return. That I would be killed. They told me to accept they would be safer if left on the street. They would be better off sleeping under a bridge and this would be a better choice than to return to hell, to death. They would rather have nothing than return to him. They wanted me to stay with them, but were ready to let me go.

I listened. I didn't understand, but I listened. I heard them and wanted to understand. I wanted to but was confused. My children meant everything to me. Everything. I could never leave them. They were leaving me. No. I couldn't be without them. No. I couldn't return to Alen. No. I wouldn't. Without my children I was nothing. Without my children I had no reason to go back. They were ready to fight for themselves and for their lives. I heard them, they would never return and offer themselves to death. No. I would not leave my children. I was beginning to understand. They were right. It was dangerous. All of my efforts through the years were wrong. I was wrong. They didn't have to say it. I felt it. I was so wrong. And so I continued to ignore Alen's texts.

By Boxing Day, I was exhausted. I was so tired but had energy all the same. Alen had sent a text the night before accusing me of not allowing 'the' kids to talk to him. Guilt. I knew this wasn't true. My kids took the opportunity to remind me of many untruths. Many stories we had to pretend to have lived. Many stories we would convince outsiders to be true, nothing but true. As outrageous as the stories at times would be, no one questioned them any longer. Most would even say, "well nothing surprises me when it comes to you guys anymore!". Many would ask, "any more excitement to share?". Yes,
so many stories but now, my kids explained, I no longer had to believe his stories or live them. My kids alone chose to ignore his text. I did nothing. "We don't have to live his story, Mom," they said. Yes, they were right. I understood.

This morning, the day after Christmas, Alen began to text again. With no reply from me, he was again back to guilt and I could see through his words, feel his frustration as this would be the first time in our history that I hadn't returned within a day. His tactics now would be confusing to me. This would be the first time I hadn't responded immediately. This was the first time for many things to come. I had no training for this. I was unprepared. The only confidence within me now was that I wouldn't leave my kids. My kids wouldn't go home. I would have to figure out a way to have Alen accept this and somehow convince him that this was in his benefit. Somehow, I had to be his friend, so that we could quietly go away and begin a new life. I was so tired and confused. Almost to a point of feeling crazy.

I AM Lucy

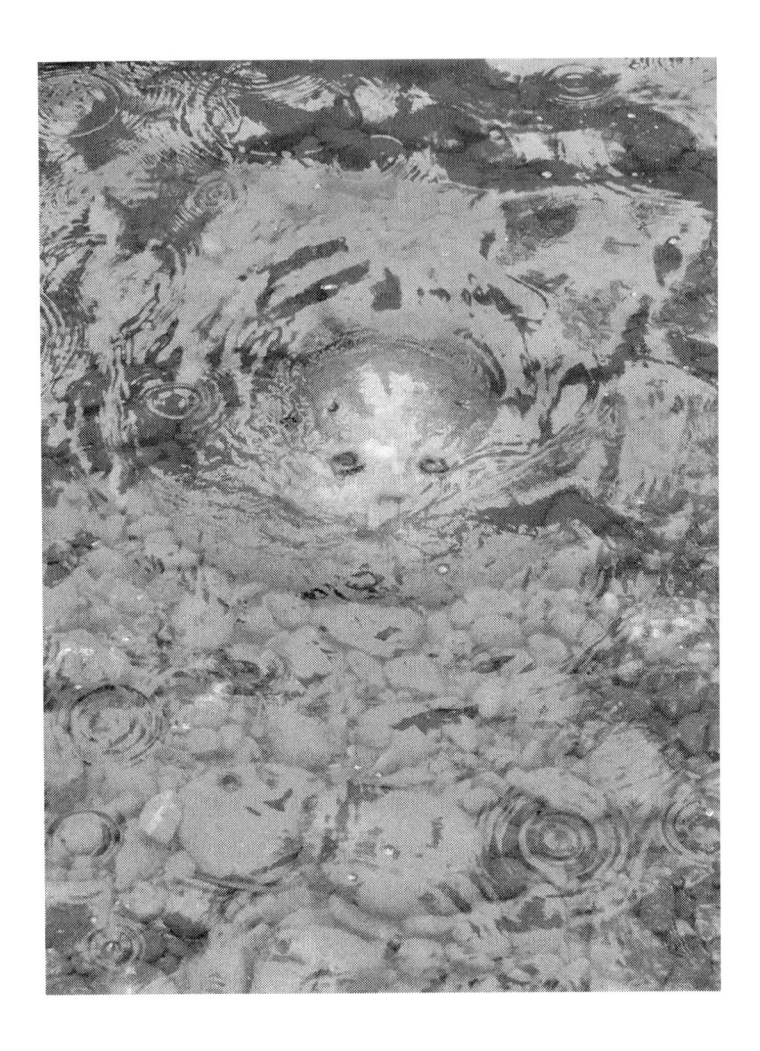

Creek by Fallen Timber, AB.
Photo by © Lucy Smolcic 2019

20 PART TWENTY
I COULDN'T TELL THEM THE TRUTH

I was fighting myself, my thoughts and Alen's voice within my mind instructing me to return. No. I wouldn't. My kids were right. I woke to a fear I recognized too well. My parents, they would call. Worse, they would visit. Christmas passed without a word from me, from my kids. They would make the drive out to the farm. I had to stop them. I knew them well. They would always check. They would never accept such silence. I drove to their house with my stomach burning and thoughts racing. What would I tell them? How would I explain? I couldn't tell them the truth, but what do I say? Alen would know if they knew too much. Alen would know. He had no empathy for anyone. He had no compassion for anyone. He would protect only himself. What do I do?

My parents were relieved to see me and immediately asked where I had been. They were going to be heading out to the farm that evening. They said they hadn't heard from us. I knew. I knew they would have driven out. My heart raced even thinking of what they would have encountered. What could have happened. I was grateful I came. I was so grateful I made it in time.

I quietly explained that Alen and I were separating. I told them not to worry and that I was simply tired of him disrespecting me and I worked far too hard for too long. I was tired. My parents understood quickly and asked if he had ever hurt my kids or hurt me. *Of course not*, I insisted. No, but the kids were now old enough that I could leave Alen and they felt it was the right decision. I explained Alen wasn't safe but had not hurt us yet. I was leaving before anything should happen. Of course, my dad readied himself to drive over to the farm and insist Alen leave so my children and I could have a home, a safe place and him and I could work on the divorce. Alen should be the one to leave the home. This was the only option my parents would consider. I was in a panic within myself yet trained to not show fear. Don't show panic. Don't show anything but calm reassurance.

It took some time, but my parents agreed to stay away from the farm. Away from Alen. Away from Alen's parents. I reassured them that he was quite angry and wasn't taking it very well that my kids and I had left. I reassured them that we would be alright and had a place to stay. I insisted they never go to Alen or his parents and even stated I would return to my life of disrespect with Alen should they break their promise. They agreed. They would give me the time to figure things out and trusted that I would make whatever decision was right, for myself and my kids. They promised they wouldn't go to the farm. They wouldn't call Alen or his parents. They would give me time to figure things out.

They gave me whatever cash they had with them and offered for us to stay. I declined, of course, as I had already explained I made arrangements. They never needed to know my car was now our home and had been for days. They would never have to suffer any guilt for not seeing things, recognizing signs or whatever I had understood from those news clips Alen had so often shown me. Proving to me the abusers were free while their victims in graves. Their families to never forgive themselves for not saving them. Not seeing the truth. Not seeing through the lies. Believing the excuses that seemed so reasonable all those times they questioned. No. I was going to quietly go away. I would figure out a way to ensure everyone was safe. Everyone. I left. I drove and parked in Airdrie.

Now what? I had begun to reply to Alen's texts and tried to keep conversation. As he sent texts explaining he was going to sell everything, including his guns and collect money for me, I replied stating he could simply take all of that money and it would be more than enough to cover the debt, pay the outstanding property tax and live comfortably for quite some time. The guns alone would accomplish this for him. I explained which bills were automatically debited from our account and which he had to manually pay. This was ignored as even though I had hope, he hadn't meant a word. His tactic was intended to have me rush back to save his dream and his guns and the life he loved so much, as I always had done in the past. To pity him and return to ensure he was alright and cared for. I grew more tired yet with this, I understood even more of how I could never return to this life. *But how would I afford to stay away?* He was so dangerous, and I had always returned. *What would he do now?* Maybe, just maybe, he really was sorry. Maybe, just maybe, his dream really meant nothing without me, without us. Maybe I could reason with him. Maybe he was ill. Maybe there was some underlying issue we could seek treatment for to help him. Maybe. Maybe he would finally get help.

I would never have believed that there would come a day when I would not understand these thoughts whatsoever. I wouldn't have been able to imagine that I would one day be ready to fight him harder than I fought any other legal battle in my past. Had I known, I would have simply ignored him. Moved on. Left.

His focus on money and selling everything wasn't the real issue. He was mentally ill and he was dangerous. He was going to kill us. He would never put this in words to be traced. Never record his voice saying those words. Never leave a trace. We were all trained. If ever he had, delete and delete again. I would sooner destroy my phone before leaving any trace of his rages. His accusations. His threats. So rare did he leave a trace, but never had I disobeyed his instructions to destroy it. Until the past year. The past year that I was waking up. Fighting myself. Screaming within my mind to do something. So these texts as well, as difficult as it was to disobey my training, were kept. All were kept. We continued.

I made an attempt to wake him up from this two-decade dream. I told him I had never asked for money. I told him our kids weren't texting him back because this was *their* choice. I asked him how he didn't see how much he had hurt them. I told him that when he wasn't angry, he was amazing. I told him how to get car insurance. Yes. All in one text.

He responded with so much yet so very little all at once. He wasn't sorry the kids had hurt 'feelings'. I wouldn't know it at the time, but he chose words and phrases that to an outsider, they would believe I only wanted money and we cared not at all for him. We used him. We were spoiled. We didn't have values. He said so much. He stated he would sell everything and the only money he would need would be a small amount. This amount he would give to his parents so they could at least have an apartment somewhere. He could 'rest in peace'. We had made him feel useless. We used him. He said a lot. Most was simply repeats of many things he would say to us all the time. Nothing really new. Nothing I hadn't already heard many times before. He advised me 'not to spend any money. To get out of the hotel'. My only response to all of this was, we were not in a hotel. He said, "still, same advice".

By 9:00pm, after I went silent and seemed to accept all that he typed, his accusations and his role as a victim, he text again. Now he asked if I would simply come home to help him, to coexist. My life at this point was chaos. My kids had already made their choice and I would not change their minds, nor did I want to any longer. The extra day away gave me more clarity but I struggled understanding why I had his voice, the guilt, trying to make me go back. *In my own head*. These thoughts must be what I truly think. They're my own thoughts. He was nowhere near me. I myself hardly knew where I was. *Go back to him. He needed my help. He wouldn't hurt me.* He was accepting of the end to our marriage and simply needed help to sell things. My kids would be alright if I left them now. I believed them. I could return on my own and send them money somehow. Provide for them, somehow. I could do this. If I didn't, I wouldn't be able to provide for them at all. I was in no position to help them. I had nothing. I had no idea how I would help them if I didn't return to the farm. I had to safeguard my children.

Kris could handle himself. He was smart. He was so smart. He was stronger than Alen. He was so strong. I knew he would take care of himself and needed to be free. Free from the torture I had put myself through and fought to overcome. He needed to be free from my guilt and the imminent torture awaiting him should he ever return to the farm. Yes. Let's split up. This would be safer. We had our own coded words. We would know how to communicate safely. No one else would understand. I let him go. I was devastated within but I could no longer expect my own son to continue suffering for me.

Now, Mia and I sat in my car and all she asked of me was for me to sleep. I couldn't. I couldn't quiet my thoughts. The words were scrambled and I felt sick. I was so sick. I was trembling. I needed to return to the farm as there was something there that I needed. I had no idea what it was, but I needed it. I felt so sick. I couldn't sleep. Mia sat beside me and patiently waited through the battles that coursed through me.

Marija. My oldest sister Marija. I had no choice. I had to call her. She would know how to tell me how to quiet my thoughts so I could sleep. I needed to help Mia and the only way to do this now, was to agree with Mia that I needed to sleep. I just couldn't. I wanted to. I really did. I just couldn't. Marija would know. I had no choice. I trusted Mia and knew she was right, but something simply wouldn't let me, let go and fall asleep. I knew it was I either call Marija or I was ready to go back. Mia, now relieved, agreed. She was all alone trying to help me, and I was alone trying to justify my thoughts to her. She was smart. So smart. Yes, she kept time moving. Kept me with her. Hour by hour. She was patient and I listened. She was calm and I listened. I still sat with her, but my mind and body desperately needed the farm.

Marija. Yes, Marija met us in a parking lot within no time at all from messaging her. She was there. She was calm. She was calm and quiet. She listened. She asked. She listened. I lied. I said some truth then lied again. Then cried and cried again. I was quiet. I was sick. I finally agreed to go to her house, where she said I'd be safe and that Mia would be safe. She kept repeating sleep, bathe, eat. Sleep, bathe and eat. Three crucial things I needed to do before making any decisions. She reassured me that Alen would be fine. He would be ok. For now, sleep was needed. I needed to bathe to feel refreshed and able to think. I needed to eat. Yes. I agreed. One more night would be fine. I could do just one more night.

Three days after fleeing. I finally slept. I bathed. I ate. I was feeling ill regardless, but I had slept. I felt clean. My body had nutrients even though I hardly cared for it. Another day of texts. These texts were now out for blood. They were out to destroy me. I was at fault for everything. I was not a woman nor was I ever womanly. I was pathetic. I used him as a tool. My kids used him. My dad used him. His own parents used him. All of our neighbours used him. All of them did. My sister used him. Everyone used him. Everyone always had and always would. He was everyone's tool. He was married to "the most non feminine female in the world" and it "took strength to love her". Pages and pages of text. So much. So many triggers. I couldn't think and was nauseated. He begged to see the children just one last time to "say goodbye". Alen, a man who never allowed those two words to be spoken. Never say goodbye unless you mean it. Unless you will never be again. Pages of text only to end with, "where do I return the movies?".

> FRI 4:46 PM
>
> Mia please contact tata hi is on live chat hi is going to kill him self please please

21 PART TWENTY ONE
THE SILENT ONE GOES CRAZY.
THE CRAZY ONE GOES SILENT.

Friday, December 28, 2018. And so the day began with my mind in another whirlwind, a tornado of thoughts and guilt, anger and sadness. I was so emotional I wanted to disappear and hide forever. I replied to Alen and tried to explain that I thought he had a substance abuse problem. I begged him to see reality and what really happened not only on the night we fled, but throughout all the years before. I received more confusing words only adding to my distress.

Finally we reached an agreement and were texting rationally. This is what I believed. We had a break though. We were civil to each other. He agreed that I can come pick up necessary items the kids needed. He seemed to understand when I explained that we only had a week to sell some items and that I only needed enough to find a small place to rent so our kids could finish school. It was still Christmas break and we had some time. A week to either sell things or, I said, we would have to move back home which meant Alen and his parents would have to find other arrangements. I asked that we stay focused on our kids as priority.

Finally, we agreed I would return this day, without the kids, to collect needed things for them and Alen would ensure he wasn't at home when I did so. As we communicated the plan, he wrote saying things had changed and he would have to remain at home as someone would be coming to the house to buy one of our items. This was good news. We agreed that I could come the following day instead and this would be alright. Our last text to each other, 2:02pm.

2:05pm. Relief. I felt relieved. Alen was now in agreement that I alone would come by and that he wouldn't be home when I did. We would work this out in favor of our children. For the sake of our children. When this was finally achieved, Mia and I agreed that attending our very first Al-Anon meeting would help and would quite possibly also help us to understand the guilt and confusion I was experiencing. Finally, my first Al-Anon meeting. Things would be alright. Yes.

2:34pm. Texts started to come in. We drove towards Calgary and we still had to wait for a couple of hours before the meeting would start, my phone was sounding off repeatedly. Texts. Lots of them. Messages. I told Mia not to look at my phone and I would check it all once I parked. Not to worry. We were doing the right thing. We didn't deserve to be unsafe. We would focus on working on ourselves and understanding these feelings and things would be much better once we had some of their belongings, or even moved back home with Alen and his parents moved out.

3:40PM. I parked, picked up my phone and my world returned to chaos. My stomach was so nauseated that I opened my door for air and struggled to remain calm. Mia questioned. What was happening? Who text? Why was I so sick?

It was all a lie.

When would I ever learn? What would it take for me to wake up?? Why had I been so stupid? So wrong? So loyal to such a demon? Why?? How had I simply ignored that we escaped with our lives just days earlier and I believed he was truly ready to do what's best? Where did my common sense go? Simple logic? All the years of evidence that he was never truthful or ever wanted to help us and I still believed him regardless.

As Mia and I sat and looked at my phone, it seemed the messages were endlessly coming in. Even one was too much! Just one. There should never have been even one. This should not be happening!

Alen was on Facebook Live. He was going to kill himself. He blamed me for ripping his children away from him. He called me a gold digger. He accused me of spending all of his hard-earned money, leaving him broke for years. He begged for his children to contact him. He pleaded for me to allow our children to contact him and to stop brainwashing them. He accused me of cancelling his life insurance without his knowledge. This is what we were *reading*. This is not what we saw or heard.

Alen blocked both Mia and I from Facebook and there would be no way to see this live chat on our own, not that we would ever even want to. Not that we would ever even need to. This performance was not intended for us to watch. It was intended for the community, the public, for them to reach out to me and guilt me into returning, *with my children*. And so they did. They reached out and begged me to allow my children to speak with their father. They included me in message groups that were filled with desperation and statements like, *"Oh dear Mother of God, save him!"* and, *"What's taking the RCMP so long!!?"* Had they known Alen blocked my kids numbers and my own that day, yet kept watching his phone as though waiting for a call from them, would they still try and convince me to bring my children back to him? Had they known he nearly killed us Christmas Eve, what would they be thinking while watching his drama unfold, live?

This is when my life changed. This is when *everything* changed. This was now something we would never be able to escape. There was no longer the ability to go quietly into a new life to escape our deaths. Now, everyone was in danger. They actually believed him. They really did. Whatever he was saying, whatever he was doing, how ever he may have appeared, they believed him! I screamed! I screamed and anger rushed me with force! This finally broke his spell on me as I read others believing his claims, his words. I saw it clearly and would never, ever have it in me to overlook his evilness again. His darkness. Finally, so clear that I would never again be with him. Reaching out to the public so they could play a role in my children's deaths. Their murders. This was now, never going to be undone. He would never again have my support, protection or obedience. Never.

This performance was the first of its kind to have ever reached the public. The Trio had never before wanted to involve anyone in their misery. They always kept up their successful, happy and wealthy appearances. They would never show they had any iota of negative, until this day. Now they had reached their own desperate moments. Now they had reached out to the world to show me, prove to me, they would win. They would always win. Their message to me was clear, regardless of how others believed what they were seeing and hearing. I understood it and it wasn't meant for anything other than to bring my children back, and to bring me back for good.

My kids and I knew far too well his stories. His games. Their games. Their stories. His ability to be someone he wasn't, along with them. To convince. To self-preserve. We didn't have to see anything, but he made sure we couldn't.

He planned this. The texts earlier were nothing but a decoy. A pause button he pushed so I would be caught off guard. Nothing more than even more lies.

"Please Lucy, let the kids talk to their Tata!"
"Oh dear God. Has someone called the RCMP?"
"The RCMP are on their way."

So many messages. Not one. <u>Not one single message asking me</u>, how are the kids? Are your kids ok?

Alen, the silent one goes crazy.
Lucy, the crazy one goes silent.

Before and after photos of our entrance in Conrich 2013.

Looking back, there were many reasons to flee yet I still stayed. In 2013, just before Alen, Mara and Kreso decided to move us all to the farm by Sundre, there had been high concern for security on Alen's part at our property in Conrich. His odd behavior and a harmless break in into my H2 resulted in a 6' chain link fence with electric gate and intercom system purchased and installed on our 4-acre property within 5 days of his decision to do so. This was a very rushed decision and although I may never understand it, his safety was of great concern for him. The harmless break into my Hummer was some sort of message to him. All that was taken from my vehicle was a tiny change purse, possibly only a few dollars' worth of coins. All valuables were left untouched. The Hummer was left untouched. Only enough was done to ensure we saw and understood someone had 'breached' our space. RCMP were not called as per Alen's instruction but the fence was immediate and kept everyone out and 'us' in. The decision to move and include his parents in this move was made by the Trio very soon after this time. I knew there was danger, I just never knew to what extent. Back then, I didn't look for answers.

To be honest, I still wonder whether this was a warning from someone he messed with, or, a set up he did himself to justify locking us in and everyone outside, out. It doesn't matter anymore. The signs of life preparing to get even worse were evident but I ignored them all. I followed his rules and ensured my children did as well.

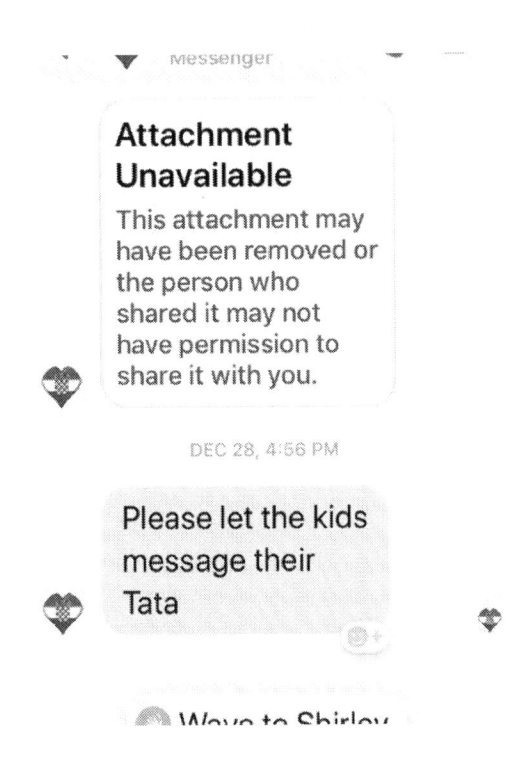

> **Attachment Unavailable**
> This attachment may have been removed or the person who shared it may not have permission to share it with you.
>
> DEC 28, 4:56 PM
>
> Please let the kids message their Tata

22 PART TWENTY TWO
ONCE UPON A TIME: THE TRUTH AND NOTHING BUT THE TRUTH

We called Kris to let him that people might be looking for us and to stay in hiding no matter what anyone might say to him. He had no intention of ever going back to the farm and told me not to worry. He'd stay safe and stay away from Alen, he asked me to promise we would do the same. This was easy. There had never before been such strength in my decision to never return home.

Alen was enlisting help from others now, to lure my kids back to their deaths. This was now clear. Finally clear. I had no more doubt. No more doubt at all. If Alen were to die now, *I would be relieved*. We would finally be safe. But I knew this was not an option and was nowhere near his plan, regardless of what he was portraying to the Facebook public. Alen was putting on a performance and my only concern was that people were now part of the dangerous life we hid for so long. We knew he had no intention of self-harm, suicide. His mission only involved the return of his children so he could silence them, as he had said on Christmas Eve, they would be gone forever.

He wasn't concerned about my escape as I wasn't a threat. He knew I would never talk. I didn't have it in me. I was just a wife, just Lucy. But his children, he needed them to be silenced. Kreso and Mara needed them to be silenced just as much. They all knew Kris and Mia weren't like me and they weren't conditioned like me, and although the trio tried their best to enforce the same control on them, they never truly succeeded.

Now, Alen desperately needed Kris and Mia back so he could finish what he set out to finish Christmas Eve, his parents too were part of this plan. This grandiose performance. The Trio had to get the children back. This was a plan between them. This would work, they believed. Kreso I'm sure, the quietest of all, either created it or at the very least, gave his approval of it and sat back to watch the show. Mara would play her part well and believed in her son's ability to put on one of the greatest shows yet. He would definitely enlist more soldiers for their plight. They were so confident, but they were also, so wrong. They were right in knowing they would enlist more soldiers, they were wrong in thinking this would be enough to bring me back. They were wrong to think my kids would ever go back. Their show did accomplish something for us though, it finally brought me on board with my kids one hundred percent. It finally brought me clarity and knowledge that this was far more dangerous than I wanted to believe.

As the stage was set and players played their parts, Mia said she needed to go for a walk to try and deal with her anger on her own and this was what she said she needed to do. She left and I trusted she would be alright. She survived far worse than this and anger was a completely rational feeling we were now allowed to feel. I waited. I waited in my own anger. My phone kept clanging its notifications that I had more messages.

Then, my phone alerted an incoming call. Mara. It was Mara now calling me. I let it go to voicemail. She, I'm sure, was positive this performance would force me to return, children alongside me. She had to make sure she helped her son as for some reason, I wasn't running back or calling her to beg for him to stop the insanity. The community should have had an effect on me. It should have already forced me to give up and force my kids back. I had no use to hear from her. My kids were safe and I thanked God for it. The only way to continue to keep them safe was to stay hidden.

Mia returned and assured me she felt we should not forego our Al Anon meeting. There was no better or more important time to attend. As I grew angrier with the community I grew up with, with every minute that passed, Mia refused to allow me to be angry with them. She said it wasn't their fault that they didn't know the truth. She told me they were being people, human, reacting to the only knowledge they had. They saw a man in despair and they naturally wanted to save him from suicide. I loved Mia for having such a beautiful way of looking at this, at this awful portrayal of ignorance. She had empathy for people she had never even met. But what she didn't know and that I was just finally realizing was, *it was their fault!* It was but not for the reasons I believed at the time.

I couldn't help but feel anger. Mia didn't grow up with these people. She was never a part of the community, the *cult*. She didn't understand that I knew, I knew they would believe him and it wouldn't simply end once they realized he survived this 'suicidal' event. They would shower him with attention. I knew attention was only going to give him and his parents the refueling they so desperately now needed to continue their sick plight to kill my children, to silence them. I knew that even those who would stay quiet, would never ask for the truth. It would have to simply go away and be buried. They would not question. None of us ever did.

I wished Mia could understand that this was far beyond a community who felt they were helping. It was a community that supported the evil. Supported the wrong. Supported the sickness that allowed so many to suffer and never question. *Never question.* They would not even question any of it. Those who would stay silent and not involve themselves, would simply stay silent. They wouldn't question other than behind closed doors and very quietly. It was all so clear now. My community, the community I knew so well all my life, were so conditioned that they wouldn't and didn't even ask. Yes I was angry. Mia still insisted I was wrong and that if I already knew all of this to be true, that they wouldn't even question or would simply remain silent, then I too was *just like them* and had no right to be angry.

This was true. Yes, she was right. I had no right. I was just like them. I was worse.

I had never spoken such words until this day. She was right. *How could I defend myself when what she said was so right? How would they have known?* I never told them. I never showed them. But I never could! My mind was a mess and thoughts scrambled in and out and clashed with each other through my chaotic mind. There would have never been a point in telling them! Nothing would have happened. No one would have helped. It had to be kept silent and hidden. This is what we knew, without ever questioning it. We just knew.
This was insanity! All of it. It would never end. *Oh God why can't I just disappear instead!?!* Back and forth my thoughts raced. *How? Why?*

Thinking back, we were all just like each other. We all never questioned. Never spoke out. Never thought to ask, anything. I remembered how Alen was so proud when he received his first unregistered handgun from an elder, a man within our community. This 'man' who beat his wife and kids as we grew up. This 'man' who drank alcohol constantly, even while out hunting with more members of this community we belonged to. This had never before even been a thought even to me, until this day. This was never mentioned. Never. Alen accepted this gift and felt as though he earned it. He bragged about it when he came home from this ceremonial meeting. This disgusting display of sickness passed along and shared with each other. He was now a 'man'. He was now accepted as one of them. So proud. He kept it close at all times. I never questioned it. Never. Not even that it was so tiny that he could conceal it and no one would ever know. He often did, and no one ever knew. I would rarely know myself. It was only the days he whipped it out to point it towards me that I knew. It was always loaded. Always.

I stayed silent throughout my childhood and into adulthood. I never spoke of what I heard, what I saw. What I knew to be awful things, wrong things. I remained silent. I never told anyone. The victims never told anyone, other than the few that would remain silent with them. It's just how it was and would be. I never questioned it.

A photo I took in Sundre, AB while walking to clear my thoughts. 2019.

23 PART TWENTY THREE
WRITING THIS BOOK

During my time in writing this very book, my first book, I posted my entries on Facebook as I wrote them. I posted of families abused, children molested and more. I posted these things and made my statement and no one else needed to, unless they wanted to. No one else had to stand up and say that these horrible things had actually happened. I did it. I said it. I put it out there for the world to know.

From childhood to that very day, at 45 years old, I knew so many of our community's secrets and yet, I was silent too. I did nothing. They did nothing. I was sure there were some who did try to do something, but nothing came of it. None of the abusers ever were charged. None of the abusers were ever shunned. None of the abusers were ever exiled. The devils we grew up with were free to continue their lives, unaffected by their awful acts. They were the devil yet made us believe we were always to blame for any wrongdoings. Anything bad that happened was somehow always our fault and not theirs. This is how we grew up. Watch what you say and do, how you act and what you wear, but those who committed crimes were untouchable. We were always being watched and always being judged while the criminals were safe. When we were all 'in line' with the rules, there was peace and acceptance. The stage was set without even understanding how we all played our roles. We wouldn't speak of it. It wasn't even a thought to question it until I began my escape from abuse. Until I began my chaotic journey trying to find answers to the questions I never bothered to even ask myself.

Those who eventually left our community were whores. They were sluts. Only the females were shunned and hated. As soon as they left they were exiled and labelled. They were the evil ones, not those devils that destroyed their spirits or crushed their hopes. Of course not. It was blamed on children. Youth. Never the 'men'. Those who left our community were turning their backs on the community. They were simply the evil doers. Yes. But again, we all accepted and stayed quiet. Never standing up for them and screaming out, they were kids! *They weren't whores!*

So many would never leave as they knew, they would be horrible people and they were raised better than that. Those who remained, never spoke out or said a thing. They were happy to be accepted and never judged. There of course is the possibility they truly never knew how sick the community was, as a whole. But there would perhaps be one day when they would start to see it. Start to question it. Perhaps. I'm sure though that it was a happy peace knowing they were safe. Safe from the cruelty the others would inflict on them should they leave or the judgment they would feel should they choose a different path that led them away.

So many suffered in silence and some never even knew there were so many others, just like them. That they weren't alone. No. But hush. Breathe. Stay quiet. As long as it's far away from me…. from us….. I'm safe, we're safe.

Oh God, my thoughts felt crazier than ever before.

We were told how to act, who to be friends with and how to dress. Yes. We were destined from birth to fit in, to conform and to stay. Marry into the community, the community would whisper. Stay with us and you will have freedom. You can drink. You can smoke. You can be free. Just stay. Don't leave. Hush. Just stay quiet and follow, or you will suffer forever and feel the shame. And even those who left and were shunned, remained quiet. I was one of them. Yes, I left and stayed quiet. I had only hoped and wished for the judgment to go away but it never would. Never because I didn't even understand what it was, until I began my true escape and began to write and explore my true self. Everyone remained quiet. Shhhhh. Hush. Never say a word. Let it stay far away…. As long as it was far away, we are safe.

It wasn't our parents, it was all parents. It wasn't me, it was all of us. It wasn't the Priest, it was the whore who left. It wasn't the judgment we never understood yet constantly felt, it was our wrongdoing that gave us this grief. Yes. I never spoke. Even when I knew it was wrong, I never spoke. It would be crazy. I would be shunned. I would be cut off from the community I always carried with me in my heart, my mind and my being.

Even when the 'new' Priest came, he was out for fear and order. He needed control. Yes, control. Not a place to come together and feel better and rejoice. That was some falsehood I used to hear through life. The funny fantasy that communities and churches were meant to build each other up, not instill fear, order and control. Not ensure eternal damnation. This new Priest could threaten a bride-to-be at any given moment to ensure she followed his every command, his every whim, his every wish to control her. Only her. I could be wrong but in over forty years, I had never heard the guys complain about our community's 'leaders' harassing them, threatening them or calling them at home to shout as they missed a service. I could very well be wrong. But even if that were the case, then these leaders were even worse than even I knew them to be. This new leader of ours would judge those who didn't marry into our community and made life holy hell for them. Yes. He would judge them. Tell them their marriages would never last so they should simply not marry. They should never marry outside the community. After all, there were so many members who belonged to our wonderful community all across Canada and in this world. We should make better choices. Yes.

Even I was threatened and judged. Even I, marrying into our community and to one who everyone knew was destined for me. Yes, even I was yelled at so many times before the wedding day. Threatened. By this leader. I was the female after all who had to *suffer for the man*. I had to prove my worth and the man could do no wrong. Yes. The Priest could cancel the wedding at any time if I didn't attend each and every Sunday, offer my money and smile for all. Alen didn't have to, but I did. It would be *my* fault if we couldn't marry in the church. I was the one who had to smile and allow myself to be treated like shit.

And so it never happened. Nothing. We were a close, tight-knit community and proud that we were. We had a bond. Individual families weren't the problem. It was the collective. It was the silence we all kept.

Yes, Mia was right. I had no right to be angry. How would these people know any different? We were all so conditioned to hear the man, the one who had no shame. We were so conditioned already, from childhood, to never question or ask for reason. No reason was ever needed. No, we were to accept. We were to support. We were never to question. And as long as it was far away, the grumbling, the problem, we were safe.

It wasn't the Fathers, it was always the crazy Mothers. It was never the guys, it was always the girls. It was never anyone because nothing was ever wrong. The men could drink. They could gamble. They could beat on their families. They could do *anything*. Of course, not all of them did but those men who didn't, stayed silent too. Nothing to be done. Leave it alone. The cycle would never be broken. Never.

Or would it?

My mind was now accepting that the community I grew up in taught me and taught the viewers of Alen's Facebook Live Chat performance, not to search for truth or answers. To simply bandage the problem and feel good in doing so. It wasn't only within our community we learned this, although it played a huge role. It was at school. It was at work. It was through the news. It was *everywhere*. The feeling we would be judged if we spoke the truth. The fact that those who spoke lies would be the stronger ones and would always win. The fact that people would be hurt behind closed doors, and we would allow it to remain there. It was everywhere. If we spoke of abuse, we were at fault. Things can only happen if you let them and if you were to speak out, to stand up for either yourself or others, you would pay the price. The abuser wouldn't. The devil wouldn't. The leaders wouldn't. It would be us, the innocent who paid the price.

I AM Lucy

I AM Lucy

Through my thoughts and realizations, I learned that we can be abused at church, at school, in a back alley, after the bar or even in a playground. But somehow, we *deserved* it.

Pictured above, he tickles and plays with a fox he just killed not knowing I had video on. This is simply one snapshot. The only times he laughed or had a genuine smile were the times he tortured us or an animal and he felt 'in control'.

24 PART TWENTY FOUR
SEARCHING FOR THE ROOT CAUSE OF WRONG

I understood more and more and as I understood more, I fought to make sense of it all. Understanding more often brought such sadness. It brought with it more questions not of the world around me, but of myself. There were days I fought to want to wake up and face another day now knowing everything was in my control and always had been. My thoughts were scattered yet made complete sense at the same time. No matter where my thoughts went, I found patterns and saw things so very differently. Things were beginning to make sense but at the same time, it was extremely difficult to deal with the guilt I constantly felt for so many of those very things. Seeking answers on my own and within my thoughts. I had never done this before and was almost scared of such new ways to evaluate life, society and my upbringing. As I began to delve into my own self and search for a way to free myself, I struggled to stop from falling further into despair. *How had I failed to see these things before?*

Knowing my son since the age of nine made constant and daily attempts to get me to run away with him and his sister. Knowing the only time him and I ever argued was my insistence on staying with Alen in order to save their lives. Every year that passed, he tried that much harder and stood up to the monster that much more. I used guilt, I used shame and I used many other meaningless excuses to convince him to not only stay, but to obey and remain quiet. The danger of my son doing something that I would fully understand, but the law would never allow, was getting closer and closer. He was ready to take matters into his own hands, and he had every right to. Looking back though, I fought hard to protect the monster rather than the savior.

Christmas Eve, 2018. In a quiet scream I insisted we were still safer staying than we ever would be leaving.

"Kris!! You're alive! Don't you get it!? Don't you care that you're alive!? *Please tell me you understand this!!*" My world was crashing and I felt I couldn't breathe or, I no longer wanted to. What I knew in my heart and what I spoke in desperation were two complete opposites.

His voice was clear. He had energy behind his words powered by his soul. "You think **this** is ***living***???! You think I'm alive? **THIS is NOT ALIVE!!**"

......

And so my search continued through the months after escaping. Knowing my kids were right but not knowing how to understand it, to live it and to accept it.
......

The victim must have dressed provocatively. Yes. It must be the skirt. Definitely the skirt. Those short shorts were no better. Don't even get me started on the cleavage. Wow was she asking for it with that! She was drunk. Stupid whore, should have stayed home that night with her cup of tea and all would have been much better. Why would she dress like that? And the make up? She was asking for it, really she was. She should have known better. She must watch too much tv or read too many of those silly woman magazines. She was asking for it to happen. She should shut up and understand, it was *her fault*.

We ignore those who cover themselves up and refuse to show their beautiful bodies. We all have beautiful bodies. This has nothing to do with weight, height, size. Whoever created us, each of us who exist, gave us all these beautiful bodies and we have shamed them. We have faulted them. Yes. We've learned that we can't blame the people or the world we live in who constantly judge even without being directly in front of us, pointing fingers and shaming. We can't blame the media or the conditioning *we have accepted*. No, we must blame our bodies. Why not? It's far easier than to deal with the actual issues that are only getting worse. Don't search for the actual cause, the real reason. No. We shouldn't even question any of it. We should simply understand this is the way it is, and everyone feels it too. Everyone has something they are ashamed of. Something they feel makes them a lesser person, less beautiful or handsome. Something's always wrong. It's our fault though. Keep it quiet and accept this and never question it. Never dig deep to find the reason for it.

White women who cover themselves are ignored. They must either be insecure or prudes. Which doesn't even make sense! The chicks who dress like 'sluts' deserve to get hassled and raped... but the chicks who cover up are boring and ignored! Goodness knows it's got nothing to do with judgment. It can't be that they were insulted as those around them made rude comments of their hip size or lack of ass. It must be they simply liked to be neutral, covered and blend into the background, unnoticed. Always. Everyone has their way, that's the beauty of freedom. We don't ask why. We don't care. We don't want to think that there's a reason for it, that might mean we ignored the real problem. Some do prefer it but in reality, we don't care. If they're white, they're insecure or prudes.

Brown women who cover are Muslim. Simple. We know all too well, don't we? We know that when we see two women, one light and one dark, there is a definite difference in what we believe their reasoning is and we don't question. Never question. We already know. We've already judged. The darker woman has chosen her path and will follow it. We don't care. If she's not wearing one of those scarf things around her head then she must be new to the whole Muslim thing, or too young? We don't know and we don't care. This is automatically not our problem and never will be. Thank goodness. They should have stayed where they came from anyway. Until we figure out a way to send them back, we'll simply ignore them. It's their sick culture that the woman accepts and adores. She loves it. Yes. If she didn't, she would do something about it. We don't care that within this group, there are many who are suffering. We don't know the difference and don't care to. They deserve it. And those who simply wish to live in peace and enjoy their religion, well, do it over there. Keep it away from us so we can turn around and blame you for keeping to yourselves. Yes. Don't come to my backyard, then I can accuse you of wanting your own kind and refusing to blend with ours.

The white woman with bruises, the dark woman with bruises. We judge. We stay quiet and speak of it quietly and do nothing about it. We don't search for reason. We don't care. We don't ask. We simply don't want to know. The white women must be crazy or on meth. Simple. See that tiny white chick by the big guy over there? He's looking down at her openly in the street. She's trembling. Her mascara is running and she's shaking. Look at her skimpy outfit that's practically falling off her body. Must be withdrawal. Must be a whore. Poor guy. He's angry because she's useless and needs a fix. I'm sure of it. He's so calm, not shaking at all. He's got his shit under control. Poor guy. He has to deal with her. *Good thing I don't have to.*

The Indigenous are too drunk and there's really no hope for them. They should really stay with their own kind too, just like those Muslims. Yes. Thank goodness that's already pretty much taken care of. The reservations are where they should stay. They love their booze and it's not our problem. They ask for it! They can't go without! If they really wanted to change they'd do something about it. They'd clean up and get jobs like the rest of us. They don't want to. Doesn't matter, as long as it's not here, beside me, by my house. They have options, I'm sure of it. They get everything they want and don't even have to pay taxes. They have no idea how lucky they are! They just refuse because they're just a bunch of addicts who deserve to get what's coming to them. They're just too lazy, not like us. Too lazy to get help. Those missing women they have? They probably just ran off and joined another tribe. Good riddance. Right. That's got to be it. Not my problem. *Thank God they don't come talking to me about it.*

Fat people want to be fat, otherwise they'd stop eating so damn much. Skinny people are full of eating disorders and should seriously pick up a spoon once in a while. Teens are liberals who can't even think for themselves anymore. We should simply, you know, us adults of the world, *keep insulting them and refuse to even have a discussion with them!* They're useless whiners. Yes. Of course. We don't even talk to them but we know, don't we. We know everything. No need to question.

Yes, the world we live in is this. So many ways we all play a part in the abuse towards others and towards ourselves. So many ways we allow ourselves to be abused as we allow others to be abused. We are all conditioned for it from the time we start school to the day we die. Fees, taxes, government, bullies, kids getting expelled for standing up for themselves, people not wanting to be called as witnesses so they simply don't look.... It's everywhere.

So this is me. I can scream all I want at my phone even the day Alen was on Facebook Live Chat, as people beg me to return my children to a monster, but the truth is, I am as much to blame as they are. As we all are. Every day. We've all allowed the world to become abusive towards us and we stay silent. Everyone. Everyone I know and will one day meet, everyone I will never meet yet share the same world with, has been abused and has remained silent at some point in their lives. Everyone has seen others be abused and stayed silent at some point. In so many ways we are all connected yet feel, believe, it's nothing to worry about and far away from here, from us. We are safe. What would it be like to come together, all of us, and simply talk and find the answers? I can only imagine the power we'd have but we would have to start with ourselves, so, chances are this will never happen. It's never us. Never our control. Never in our power. We've said it too many times, the power is out of our hands. And so it is. And so it will remain to be. So simple.

Those who say they speak out and aren't silent, what have they really done? Have they searched for the root cause so we can fix the problem? No. They scream about the problems. Sure. They aren't silent. Okay. But have they found the answers and the cause? Have they looked into history to find the pattern? Have they spoken with others to see what more they may learn or understand from the very basic tool we all have within our reach? Conversation? Discussion? Debate? Openness? I have a feeling they may be loud, but they are still just as silent as I've been.

I would one day be able to explain how everyone understands what it's like to have lived my life without even knowing it. I would one day be able to give examples of it and would understand it more myself. I would one day ask more questions and be determined to live true not only to myself, but to those who share this world with me. This would be the only true way to break the awful cycle. To free my own kids from continuing the cycle.

Mia and I attended our first Al Anon meeting regardless of what our lives had been thrown into this day. There were no more excuses for me to put off dealing with truth. Dealing with the fact that I was and will continue to be, a mess. I had lived far too long with abuse. My children deserved to have a Mom who took ownership of her life for once. Stop making excuses. Stop being a victim, hopeless and destined for death with no life. Stop blaming the world. Stop blaming myself. Stop blaming and start addressing the real issues. Start asking the real questions and look for the real answers. Be open to the answers, regardless of what they may be. Take ownership and solve the actual problem, not run from the symptom. I had no other choice but to look only at myself in order to deal with the reality that was my life.

We deserve to be safe. The public deserves to be safe. They had no idea how unsafe they were. They didn't even want to ask! So I would have to now, instead of quietly escaping so no one would have to know my shit and so I could rebuild a life in peace, now I had to ensure Alen and his parents could not harm another single soul in this world of ours. My kids were right. Now it was time to do what was right, not what was easier or less humiliating. It was time not only for us but for the world around us. My kids tried to tell me this for years. Years! *I never listened!*

Original Spiritual Art by © Lucy Smolcic

25 PART TWENTY FIVE
I PROMISE TO SPEAK THE TRUTH AND NOTHING BUT, FOREVER AND ALWAYS, NO MATTER WHAT

The shock. The horror. The judgment to come. Fuck them.

A family I knew, a family of four. The father was evil. He beat his wife and his children for years. He was evil. Regardless, we loved him and others like him. He was my favorite teacher. I loved him. Yes. I ignored the bruises of my friends and their Mom. I did. It must have been a playground fall or an accident. They were always so happy and full of life. Even when I knew he had hit them, they told me, I knew to be quiet. It could be worse. They were fun and we all lived in this wonderful fantasy together. Even as the children grew, they grew even taller than their father and some would say the boy should have then simply hit back. Why, if it was really that bad, didn't he simply now hit back? I remember, yes I do.

I remember everything now in a different light. I am disappointed in myself and my community of people, my world. We should have all, at the very least a hundred of us if not more, gathered and went to their home. We should have all, standing together as one, ripped this being, this so-called man, five new assholes to shit out of then very clearly told him to disappear. Yes. We should have. We should have protected those children, that woman. Instead, we were all silent. Protecting him. We acted as though it never happened, even when it never ended. Some tried to call for help and this never solved anything, did it? Those who tried, soon understood there would be no point to their involvement and attempts. Nothing ever came of it and so, what was the point? And we, the very same people have the nerve to say today, how does this happen? Why didn't you leave? We had no idea. Yes. Of course it makes sense.

Those who will shun me one day, one day when I finally do what's right and I finally speak the truth and nothing but the truth, those who stand against me can watch as I smile. I will smile and stand proud to finally say what so many wouldn't or couldn't. What I wouldn't. Or maybe they have said it and nobody listened. I sure didn't listen to even my own kids. How do we get people to listen?

What was the root cause of my own problem all along? Why had I allowed myself such a 'life'? I would one day say it and accept judgment. The day would come when I finally accepted that no one could judge me but possibly God and myself. One day, I would tell the world that it's not domestic abuse that is the real problem. It's everyone who hasn't accepted that we've all been silent. All of us. We are all so used to pointing fingers. We are so used to accepting we can't change the evils in this world and that it's far too great a mission. We would rather stay quiet, live the best we can and not search for the real answers.

One day, I would sit in a room in a house that doesn't belong to me. One day I would be typing on a floor instead of a desk with the beautiful lamp I once owned to bring light into the darkness as I write, trying my hardest to figure out a way to answer questions no one really wants to ask.

I would believe in the Spirits of the Indigenous Grandmothers who hold my hand and guide me as they protect me from those who wish to silence me. One day, I would simply write to the world who is willing to read my words and as they eagerly await more truth, I will know there will be more who would wish I remain silent. There would be more who would judge. There would be more who would question my truth and wonder if this world I explain is nothing but a story, while knowing it was all real and needed to be said. Some might say it's a story created to justify myself. Some might say, whatever they want. I wouldn't allow anyone to control my words or my actions, any longer.

I'll know that there would be many who would read these words that I type, as they cry. I'll know there will be many who will need help in coping with the fact that I told their secrets and they would be terrified, yes, terrified that I would somewhere along the line expose even more truth or even their names, the names of the victims.

I'd tell them, rest assured and be calm, you know me. Although I know many secrets, they aren't my truth to tell. It's my obligation now, as a human being, as a person who shares this world with you, to say that yes, it all happened! It's real. You're not the only one and many have shared these secrets with me through the years. Many times I simply overheard. Many times it was the nightmares you spoke of, not knowing they were your subconscious telling you the truth. You are not alone. And although your secret will always remain safe with me, it's time I say it loud and clear that it's **not your fault**. Never was. Never will be. *I will take on the world for you.*

I will be able to do this because of my kids. Because of my support. Because I never deserved to live this kind of life. I didn't even know why I lived this way until now. It would be selfish of me to keep it inside any longer. It would be wrong. It is wrong. The evil of the world shouts from high above us as we cower silently waiting for the torture to end. *This is wrong.* Let the evil crumble to our feet as we destroy it with the power of truth and the power within us. We are not to blame for the evil we had to endure. We are not to suffer so that the evil feels less threatened. We have self respect, although it's buried within most times, we need to own it. Live it. Love it. Use it. *Believe in it.*

I will know that telling my own truth brought with it freedom. I will no longer live with the feeling that I can't explain, always telling me I'm doing something wrong. I will no longer hide in the shadows with this gift I want to give others. Others will never have to speak their truth to the world if they don't want to. The decision to come out and break my silence was my own. I do not regret it. I know I wouldn't have ever come as far as I have if I remained silent. I may not even exist, if I stayed quiet. I will never know for sure if this is true but I am confident it only changed my life for the better. I'm also confident in saying, I was <u>not</u> safer being quiet. This I know for certain. This I will write about in Book Two if I don't become a statistic before then, that is.

Now that my truth has been spoken, I will own it. I will own it and show others that life isn't to be lived in silence. That's not a life. Silence is not the answer, ever. The more people knew, the safer I became. I waited four months after fleeing my violent home and reporting abuse to the RCMP's before I came out with my truth publicly. I came out with my truth to those who were friends of mine on Facebook. Social media has been used in so many ways as I've watched over the years and only in April of 2019, did I find a true purpose for it myself. Once I spoke out, my world opened up and changed. All of my doubts began to leave me. My concern of being judged became a thing of the past and I was no longer hiding behind what I felt should be my life and spoke out of what my life had really been. I spoke the truth.

Once my truth was finally spoken, I spoke of truths belonging to others. Others I would never name as I spoke out to begin to break my cycle and ensure I no longer continued the sick and painful silence I was taught to accept as normal. I spoke of what crimes I knew of through my childhood into my teenage years that my peers had to suffer. From what I knew, no one had ever told the ugliness of what had once been and could possibly still be. I spoke of molestation, violence, abuse and lies. All hidden behind fake smiles and false happiness. I spoke it for all but mostly, for myself. I had such a burden carried with me because I was a witness to such trauma to so many, and said nothing. Did nothing. This was a life we deserved. What a horrible feeling and I would thankfully, one day never, ever feel it again. That is freedom.

I carried with me so many secrets. So many evil deeds hidden in the depths of my mind. Why? Because this was what I was taught. Not by simply a mother and father, but the entire world I grew up in. Within my own community, at school, through work, everywhere I was exposed to daily abuse of others yet more often than not, all go not only unreported, but ignored and buried far deep within us. Accept it. Forget it. Move on.

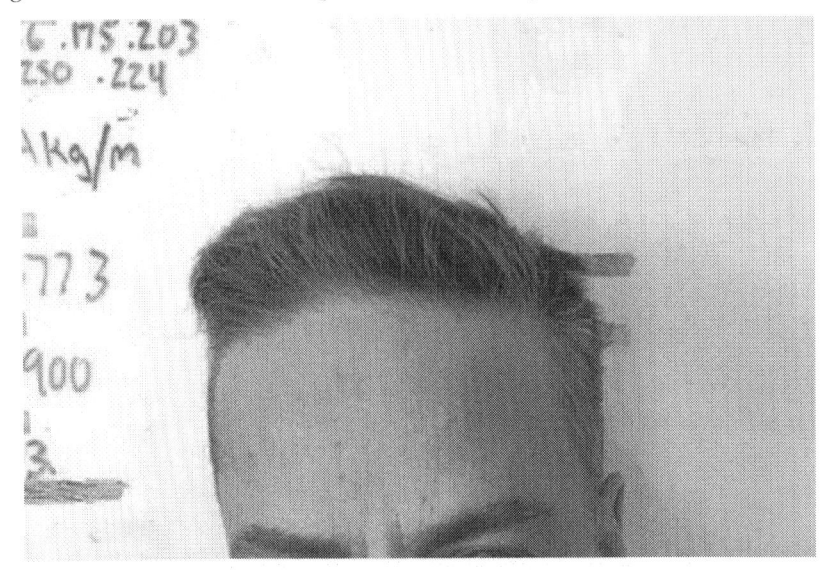

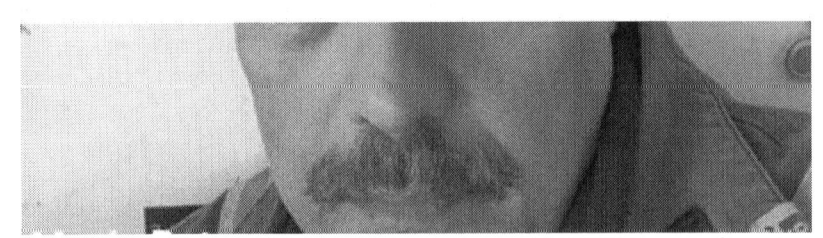

Nothing I can do. Nothing we can do. Keep that shit far away from here! From me! That's what I used to believe and it's what I used to live like. Never again. Yes, I mean never.

26 PART TWENTY SIX
RCMP DID EVERYTHING THEY COULD TO KEEP US SAFE AND I TRUST THEM. THE ABUSE CONTINUED EVEN STILL AND WITHIN THE LAW, OUR VERY OWN LEGAL SYSTEM. THIS IS TERMED LEGAL HARASSMENT AND IS QUITE SIMPLY, ABUSE SUPPORTED AND ENFORCED WITHIN THE LAW, FAMILY LAW.

Following December 28, 2018 and Alen's online Facebook stunt, the world around me closed in and I knew I had little choice left. Alen took the only thing I wanted away yet again, the ability to simply leave. To leave quietly. I only wanted to somehow find a way to just leave quietly. Now, knowing so many were involved in his play, too many were at risk and I could no longer only worry for myself. I heard he even asked a young man, early twenties, to visit him to help him and he would be a father to him. Sickness was about to spread. The danger was spreading.

I could still leave and never return. I could. But who would warn others of the danger around the farm? Who would let them know these people were capable of unimaginable evil? No. It was time to do the right thing. To have these people, the Trio, held accountable for their extreme, traumatic abuse towards myself and my children. It was time to tell the truth.

I called the RCMP. Yes, I did. I would not be able to write the details of the call, the call I made to Victim Services or the original statement I made until after the charges were brought to trial. My first book would be published well before trial began and I would have to wait for my second book to describe the charges, the abuse, the legal harassment and how I changed my life. I would not jeopardize the case and so a second book would need to be written.

What I would write about, when the time came was that I was trembling. I was sick. I felt I was dying on the inside. I was terrified. But I was ready. I had to report domestic abuse and I did. Without going into details, I would write that my kids spoke up for themselves. They both wanted to do this for years but protected me instead of themselves. They finally, finally had the freedom from my own guilt and shame to do the right thing.

With ONLY SOME incidents of abuse from May 22, 2015 onwards, Alen was charged on January 1, 2019 under the Criminal Code, RSC 1985, c. C-46 as amended with:

   a. 3 counts under s. 266 (Common Assault);
   b. 2 counts under s. 267(A) (Assault with a Weapon);
   c. 1 count under s. 271 (Sexual Assault);
   d. 1 count under s. 151 (Sexual Interference);
   e. 1 count under s. 86(1) (Careless Use or Storage of a Firearm; and,
   f. 1 count under s. 92(2) (Possession of an Unauthorized Firearm).

To note, C and D are charges the RCMP laid against Alen for Mia, not for me as many have assumed. There will be more charges for us all, but the sexual assaults were against our young daughter.

Alen was arrested and charged, then released on Recognizance on January 2, 2019. The conditions of his Recognizance stipulate that Alen is:

   a. To have no contact or communication whatsoever, either directly or indirectly with me or the children except when in court, through legal counsel;
   b. Banned from going within a 200 metre radius of any known residence of me (this includes my parents and siblings);
   c. To have no contact or communication whatsoever either directly or indirectly with the Children except when in court or through legal counsel;
   d. Banned from going within a 50 metre radius of me and the Children anywhere in Alberta;
   e. Prohibited from owning, having in his possession or carrying a weapon, including knives except those used for preparing or eating food, and work tools while he is at work; and,
   f. Prohibited from possessing a firearm, crossbow, prohibited weapon, restricted weapon, prohibited device, ammunition, prohibited ammunition or explosive substance.

The RCMP seized all weapons, guns and firearms. This too has a story behind it and will be shared in the future. Although I wanted to, I could not charge Mara and Kreso under any current law within Alberta or even

Canada. All that they had done was within the laws we live by. Had they hit one of us, had they even pushed us just once, this would be against the law. All the abuse we suffered at their hands was within the law. Even though the emotional, financial and coercive abuse they inflicted on us did in fact make us suffer physically, this is not considered assault. What in the world does that even mean?

This was something I would continue to struggle with until I found a way to hold them accountable for their abuse as well. Just as I would one day work on charges that I didn't bring forward during my initial statement out of fear and some that extended past the Didsbury RCMP's district. Just like the awful and brutal killings of two of our dogs. Both killed by Alen, both made to suffer and in no way put down humanely. Both examples to myself and my children of his capabilities of being a monster, his threats that could easily become reality and the trauma of having to live with the memories. The memories alone carry guilt. We may not have done the awful killings, but we had to know of them and be witness to them.

The weeks following Alen's arrest were indescribable. I would one day be able to tell of them in detail but would limit myself until I knew nothing would be able to affect the legal system and their ability to follow through with the charges and deal with them properly, in a court of law.

I would say though that the week following Alen's Facebook stunt left me in a hopeless state and I felt as though I would be stuck in limbo forever. Due to the holidays, law firms were all closed and I couldn't find legal advice. Most counselling was overwhelmed with calls of abuse and I was told this was one of their busiest times of the year and unfortunately, they were understaffed. It would take weeks for me to see a therapist and when I did, I was told my situation was so extreme, I would need to wait and go to yet another therapist who may be better able to deal with my needs. In the end, I finally found a therapist, my third attempt, who began to help me. I began antidepressants in January 2019 and would continue them, most likely, for over a year or so I was told by my Doctor. Ultimately, Alen cancelled my insurance and I abruptly had to stop taking them in July 2019 after being awarded my first court order for child and spousal support.

During the first few weeks following Alen's arrest and release we were still in hiding. The RCMP and I agreed that the farm would not be a safe place for us and it was isolated with numerous safety concerns. Alen had hid weapons in places on our property and this was something no one would be able to protect us from in any case. Returning to our property would only bring about worst case scenarios and the best case would be for us to simply go into hiding and be on a constant look out for him. I had every legal right to remove Alen and his parents from the property, but I would then have to return to live there. There was no legal way to remove them and not return myself. I agreed it was the safest decision to stay away from our property which meant, I gave Alen permission to remain. I had no other choice.

As part of Alen's abuse towards me was financial, I had the majority of our bills on my own name. Within the first week and for weeks to follow, Alen made attempts to call my cell phone provider Telus, and access both mine and my children's cellular information and usage. He wanted details. I had safe guarded us shortly after his release by calling Telus to notify them of my situation and instructed that they never provide Alen with any information pertaining to the three of us, but in no way stopped them if he simply wanted his own number transferred to his name. I requested they call Alen and offer him his number be transferred, even though I could have easily and legally, cancelled his cell phone number immediately. He continued to make attempts to access our information regardless of Telus informing him he could not do so. Alen lied to Telus several times saying he had sent a payment for the account, yet with each call he made, he again tried to convince the agent to give him our information. I was fully aware of each call he made to them and logged this information to have for my reference. His abuse continued.

Alen sent over 400 texts in one evening asking for character references. As I was the 'owner' of our bills, I was able to view Alen's usage in detail. This was excellent for me as I was then aware if he was in the Sundre area, Calgary area, or even northern Alberta. I would limit our travels to certain areas these days. This also allowed me to know that there were several people who communicated with Alen, multiple times, at great length, then made attempts to befriend me or tried to portray their trust and support for us, when in fact, I already knew their roles in his play. I knew which girlfriends he spoke with late into the nights, even before I ever fled, as now I searched history along with the present. I had to make sense of the chaos within my thoughts and answers were easy to find, once I looked for them. Very easy. I was grateful he refused to transfer his cell until much later. While he thought he would gain access to me and the kids, all along, I was watching and seeing everyone he spoke with, text and send photos to. I saw it all.

While Alen had been busy asking for help from the public, character references and such, the Crown has issued only three subpoenas and has never once asked me for a witness, reference or evidence. Three. Me, Kris and Mia. While Alen was busy trying to save himself, yet again, he cared not at all for his children. Those he so desperately needed that day on Facebook. Yes, those kids. Over half a year after this Facebook stunt of his, he had not once asked even through legal counsel, how the kids are, if they needed anything, or any other possible question he was legally allowed to ask through counsel. Not once. Ever. He refused to pay child support. He refused to allow us to retrieve belongings. Yes, there will be much to be written in Book Two.

The house phones were also in my name. This too helped me heal. This too helped me understand the extent of abuse I lived through and the lies these people had me live for so long. So long, that I eventually believed most of them.

It would possibly surprise those viewers who experienced trauma watching Alen, believing his words and his act, that while he earlier that day had me believe we could work this out in a civil manner and I could get some items my kids needed, he had been making calls to the bank and insurance. He spoke with his ever-loyal friend for 31 minutes between texting me. He had a plan all along. He was freezing accounts and trying to find a way to make me suffer even more. Put me in a worse position than I had already been in and force me to return. Yes, Facebook was part of the plan, his plan and he enjoyed every minute of it, trust me. He enjoyed people who suffered, animals who suffered. He is very sick. He is very dangerous.

His claim of my cancelling life insurance is false. I have evidence to prove this dating back to March 2018. His knowledge and his instruction to cancel these so he could spend more money, reminding me of how broke we always were, can easily be proven and I have the proof. Reminding me to not spend money. I have evidence, for everything. The fact he spent Over $53,000 within 6 months while sending me messages to not spend. We were broke. We had to watch 'our' spending. Of course I have evidence as I was waking up for at least a year before I finally fled. I also have evidence that he would one day reinstate these insurances, but not until the supposed surgery was scheduled for his kidney donation to his brother, the one he would only intend to do when it would most benefit him, not his brother. I have evidence of this as well. I have evidence that he had used his kidney, the one thing he could actually do to save his own brother, he used this multiple times in the past year to avoid job offers, work schedules, and so on. Yes. He also avoided testing to see if he could donate and only had the application sent November of 2018. This after my kids and I spent the year begging him to save his brother, but he was too busy. He was also too busy lying to his own brother that he had gone for testing, when in fact, he hadn't. Eventually he did, but not as early as he said he had.

The Doctor even informed Alen that he didn't necessarily have to even be a match, he could simply donate a kidney to the foundation and this would automatically put his brother at the top of the list. But again, Alen didn't want this. He didn't want to stop drinking and doing whatever else he had been doing. He didn't want to have Doctors touching him, he didn't trust them. He feared his own death. Yes. He stalled but told the world he was a hero. Always a hero.

I have evidence of the thousands upon thousands upon even more thousands of dollars Alen spent for years. All the time. Dating back to 2005, then Renalta, then China and so on. All of it was spent by him and only him. I have evidence that he had an entire group who had a contract in China, which is how Alen got his job in China, he had the entire group fired. Yes. They were fired, he remained. He did this.

Evidence that he lost a tooth and kept it in his pocket for weeks only to lie at work, saying he was hit in the cheek by a tool, so he could claim WCB and have it repaired, not on his dime. I have evidence of so many things that my list would take pages and pages to detail the evidence I have. Evidence that he was referred to mental health in 2017 and I had to work diligently to remove the referral. Evidence he lied to his current employer multiple times and hated each of them, any employer, as Alen hated to work. Evidence he hated his most loyal friend and called him a bad girlfriend and made excuses through me not to see him on multiple occasions. Evidence of so many things. But still, he continues to lie.

He continued to try and control me, even after I fled and even after the charges and even for months and months to follow. He knew he could communicate with me only through legal counsel. It was within the law. I finally found a lawyer who would be willing to accept payment by way of a lien on my property. I desperately tried to apply for legal aid as I had zero access to anything, not my home, not my assets, nothing. Legal aid refused my application stating that even though I had no access, my assets were well above their limit and I was not approved. Alen counted on me not being able to find a decent lawyer who wouldn't require payment, but I found one. And he then began his harassment of her. He harassed her and me. She withdrew. My second Lawyer would be the same scenario.

He talked down to my lawyers through each email he sent. He tried instructing them of what they had to do. He even took them to court. He increased my legal fees weekly, multiple times. He accused me of abuse. He accused me of having a history of violence. He accused me of being a bad mother. He put his own statement into the RCMP with multiple accusations. He sent my lawyer messages instructing her to instruct me to continue helping his parents. He wanted me to change email addresses for them, contact the CRA and so on. Yes. He kept abusing me through my legal counsel. All within the law. He made it so impossible to continue, the estimated cost of our divorce was originally estimated at $20,000, and within just a couple of months, this estimation was brought up to $50,000-$100,000. All due to his delays, his threats, his accusations and his refusal to deal with what the law required of him. Child support, spousal support, property and assets...

Alen stated and swore he had never, in his life, threatened or implied he wanted to kill himself. This he stated both filed with the Court of Queen's Bench in Calgary and with the Didsbury RCMP.

He tried stating that his parents owned half our property. Then he said they loaned me money. Then he said I forged documents. Then he said I hid $241,000. Then he said I stole $121,000. Then claimed I hid over One Million dollars. Then said I was never able to earn a dime. Then said I earned everything. The list of things he's falsely stated and sworn to is too long. All the while, I was trying my best to support my children. I was trying my best to heal. I was trying my best to move forward. I was trying my best to be strong. I was falling apart then picking myself back up. Only to fall again. When would I have the time to heal?? When would I have the time to focus on life in the present without having to receive yet another message of what Alen was now saying, doing or trying? When would I be able to focus on my children and their health, their mental health, their ability to move forward? When? I did it every day! No matter what Alen attempted in getting me to quit, to run, to disappear.

He wanted me to quit. Yes. Of course. He wanted the children back with him. If they were hungry and homeless, of course they would return to his control. My children would rather be hungry and homeless. My children refused to be abused any longer. His plan continued regardless. Alen's parents never contacted my children, thank God. But neither did Alen's relatives. None of them. They made no attempt to contact me or my children or to ask if they needed anything. Nothing at all. Zero. My family, my friends, and even strangers all offered support and continued to help in many ways. My parents, both seniors, helped tremendously. Alen did not. Mara and Kreso did not. All of the family on Alen's side did not even reach out, not even once. My children did not exist to them. This would be perfectly alright and we weren't surprised. This was the way they were, the abusive cycle never to be broken. Not for them at least.

My kids tried to finish school in Calgary. This didn't work well. Not only was life itself stressful and full of uncertainty, I was running into so many in Calgary who, instead of asking me if my kids were okay or needed anything, asked where they were. Where were they. Were they in Calgary? Did I live in this area? Yes. I knew they were alerting Alen. I knew our safety was never going to be a priority for them. They wouldn't even ask how they were, only where they were. Eventually, my kids and I decided that we were safer back in Sundre rather than in Calgary. Why? My kids knew no one that Alen and I knew in Calgary and between our community, the oil industry and others, we knew a lot of people. Only I would recognize threats to our location. My kids never left the place we stayed in while in Calgary. They never left. They wouldn't know if someone Alen knew was near them. But my kids knew Sundre. Sundre knew Sundre and who ever didn't belong was known and stood out to all. My kids had others who would look out for Alen and his parents as well, or any strangers, really. The teachers knew of our situation and would help. Yes, we moved back and rented so my kids could finish their semester. Yes, we were much closer physically to Alen and his parents but we were also much safer as we knew they wouldn't send people in to track us without our knowledge any longer.

Within days of our return to Sundre, Mara and Kreso sat waiting in the local burger joint, waiting for one of my kids to show up. Lunch time. Kris showed up and saw them inside, seated next to each other, facing the entrance way. They stared at him. Them in their leather jackets, Mara all dolled up with her sparkling jewels, while my kids were hungry and we could hardly afford our rent. Yes. They weren't there to offer support. They weren't there to see if he needed anything. They were there as a message. "Hi Kris!" Mara exclaimed with a smile. Kreso simply sat and smiled along. Fortunately, Kris was smart and simply left. He could have done far worse. They were very lucky he chose to leave.

All the while that Alen continued his tactics of abuse towards me and my kids, increasing legal costs and refusing to provide any support, he continued his plight on Facebook and playing his role as victim. Still, no one asked me a thing. I had only communicated with two Croatians at this time and one Canadian friend. Everyone else, zero questions. I did my part in saving the public from his craziness, his weapons were seized. And even though I knew he still had many hidden, it was far more difficult for him to simply have access to the artillery he once had within our home. Even though this was all done to safeguard those involved, they still didn't contact me or ask me anything. Eventually, they would trickle in with messages but not until I finally did my own Facebook post. Coming out with the truth. This was in April, 4☐ months following our escape. 4 months.

☐☐☐☐☐☐☐☐☐☐☐☐☐☐☐☐☐☐☐☐☐☐☐☐☐☐☐☐☐☐☐
☐☐☐☐☐☐☐☐☐☐☐☐☐☐☐☐☐☐☐☐☐☐☐☐☐☐☐

Many from my old community then offered help and clothing and anything we would need. Many people in general offered us so much help. Yes. They truly helped far more than I could ever have imagined or ever thank them for. No one asked for reasons before, but once I spoke, the offer for help was coming from everywhere. And slowly, messages started to trickle in from only some of those who had been Alen's rock, support and shoulder for so long.

As time moved on, I battled Alen's constant correspondence through my lawyer and his accusations. All the while, I had knowledge that he was announcing on his Facebook page that he was finally, healing. All the while he was attacking me, never asking about the children, not once. He had opportunity every day to ask through my lawyer, but never did. On Facebook, within his play, he was pitied and received many forms of support. While he played victim, he filed his Sworn Statement of Defense on February 21, 2019. He had it stamped and filed by the courts, handed a copy in person to my lawyer and to the RCMP. Within this statement, he refused to allow my application for Divorce stating that it was not deemed 'impossible' for us to reconcile.

He stated, just a few examples:

"At no time has Alen attempted or threatened nor has any intention on committing suicide";

"Lucy has a history of violence, abuse, compulsively lying and manipulating people";

"Lucy assaulted Alen with a garden shovel";

"Lucy has negligently left the farm animals underfed and cared for. To the point neighboring farmers and veterinary professionals expressed concern and assisted while Alen was away for work";

"Lucy has proven incompetent and negligent in being able to maintain any sense of stability in her or the children's lives. Lucy has proven with her past inconsistent work history, inability to handle her own personal affairs, lack of financial stability and zero facts or examples that would make her even remotely eligible of being a single parent".

There is much to be said of everything Alen was doing to force me to quit. To fall apart. To doubt myself. To regret leaving. None of his statements were true, at all. None. There was zero truth within them, I searched for even a shred but couldn't find even one to cling to hope. It was useless. I debated giving up, but not for long. I worked according to his every whim for *twenty years*. Everything was his choice. Everything was his purchase. Everything was him and never me. Never my kids. I never spent money. My kids never spent. We were always making Alen and his parents' priority. We were forever working on the businesses or on the farm without any benefit to ourselves, other than staying alive. We suffered physically and mentally. We were beat. We were yelled at. We were threatened. We were poisoned. We were drugged. Every day was a battle. No! I would not quit. We earned our share, and by the time this would be done, I believe we deserved not just a share of the assets and property, but all of it.

Eventually, every move Alen made to destroy me, gave me strength. Every accusation he made so confidently, gave me strength. Every Facebook post he made to ensure support, gave me strength. If only he were to have known, I became stronger than ever before. As time passed I gained even more strength through the Spiritual world. I was surrounded by people who showered me with encouragement and love. I grew more and more determined to do what was right. To search for answers. To never give up.

I would also never quit searching for a way to make Mara and Kreso accountable for their abuse and evil actions. Justice may not always be served, as I've been reminded, but there will be justice. Sometimes life brings about different forms of justice. There will be justice. Our suffering will not simply go away.

I fought for Alen and Kreso in legal cases that were impossible to win, and I won. I won because I feared not winning and feared for my life. They should now imagine, with my mind returning to 'normal' and I have full control of myself, what I am capable of doing for the right reasons. For the truth. For myself and my kids. Evidence is everywhere. Alen, Kreso and Mara cannot hide away forever. They will see their day in court. Sometimes, court isn't behind walls but out in the open for the world to be the judge and jury. Sometimes, the public court is the best justice ever served. I am ready.

I AM Lucy

Original Painting by © Marija Smolcic 2019

PART TWENTY SEVEN
A PART OF ME FELL APART BUT I AM NOT BROKEN
FREEDOM

Christmas Eve, 2018. In a quiet scream I insisted we were still safer staying than we ever would be leaving. "Kris!! You're alive! Don't you get it!? Don't you care that you're alive!? *Please tell me you understand this*!!" My world was crashing and I felt I couldn't breathe, or I no longer wanted to. What I knew in my heart and what I spoke in desperation were two complete opposites.

His voice was clear. He had energy behind his words powered by his soul. "You think ***this*** is ***living???!*** You think I'm alive? **THIS is NOT ALIVE!!**"

July 26, 2019. Seven months later. We are all living. We are not only alive, but we are living. I will never again allow fear to rule me. I will never again ignore reality and replace it with what anyone believes it should be. I create my own reality. My own life. I live by my rules. I have no more regrets. I accept my past and forgive myself. I accept my mistakes and have learned from them. I am not perfect and never will be. I will move forward, day by day, being true to myself. I am blessed to be able to say, my kids are also living day by day, being true only to themselves.

………..

I want to share something someone said to me before I begin my ending to this first book I've ever written. One quote spoken to me in January 2019.

Man says to me, "you will soon be feeling better and everything will work out. You will build a new life and be happy".

"Yes," I chuckled, "I'll have everything I ever imagined, minus the husband part!"

"Lucy, you've never had a husband. I don't know what you would call what you had, but it's nowhere near a husband."

This conversation has been on my mind many times and I never, ever would have thought of it that way. I am grateful to everyone who has taken the time to share their words, their stories and their support.

My life was not lived with a Man. My children never had a Father. A Man, a Father would never do these things and continue to do them. He would never treat other people like slaves or hurt them. A Man will protect his family, not
destroy them. I thank all the Men of this world we live in for being true Men. I will forever love Men as the thing I lived with is nothing even close to one, therefore, he could never make me dislike or distrust men. Afterall, I raised a Man and I am very proud of him. My son has proven that Men exist regardless of their upbringing or past. My daughter growing into a woman teaches me the very same. The past does not dictate who we are today. We have no excuse to become monsters, only monsters use excuses.

I AM Lucy

This is me in Vinkovci, Croatia 1994

Photo of me September 22, 2019

...EVERYTHING THAT LED TO MY COMING HERE...

......Everything that led to my coming here, to this life I now live, is all making sense. I always knew I needed to go to an extreme in life to really understand the emotions that are part of my being. I now believe everyone understands me and my intense feelings. I am 45 years old and my life has just begun. This is my first year to get to know my own children and who they really are and what their dreams may be. Regardless if they pursue them or not. It's part of who they are today and tomorrow, I look forward to hearing it all again. My children finally, this year, get to know me. They've just met me……

Thank you to all the men, women and children who have supported us.

I am ~~just~~ a **Woman**.

I am ~~just~~ a **Mother**.

I hope to one day be ~~just~~ a **Grandmother**.

I am **Lucy**.

Deal with it.

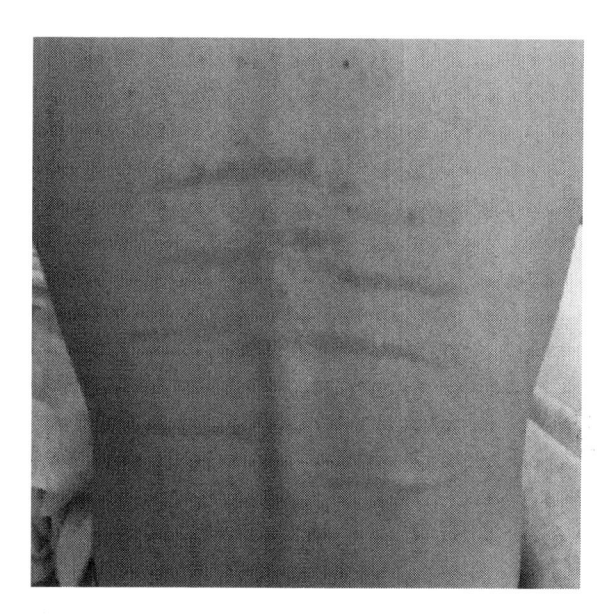

MY SON SAVED MY LIFE

An image of my son's back two years after the attack on him. This is only an image, in person you can still see the scars are several millimeters thick and the skin will forever be broken. This was the result of Kris calling the RCMP on Alen to save MY life in 2016.
Although details of this will come out during the trial, I will explain just a small portion of the true story.

Kris had a freshly broken ankle plate and although for years he always jumped in or ran to defend me and his sister against Alen's attacks whenever possible, there was one day in 2016 he could not. Outside, and witnessed by Mara and Kreso from within the house, as I was knocked unconscious. Mia was just feet away during his attack on me, Kris unable to run out to protect us in time called the RCMP to save my life. **MY LIFE** and most likely **his sister's life** as well. As you can see from the above image, Alen ensured Kris would never forget, that we all would *never forget*, how we were never to ever ask for help, call for help or make a sound.

These scars are over two years old. They still haven't fully healed. They will never fully heal but Kris will heal because he refused to continue to live in abuse and **he broke the cycle**. To this day and even in family court, Alen has insisted that these scars are *stretch marks*. There is no Doctor in this world who will support this story of Alen's. He is a monster. He needs to be held accountable for each and every act of violence, abuse and even threats to my children and myself. And he will be.

For those who still question whether to leave abuse or not. *Read this again.*

I was **WRONG**. I was wrong to ever have stayed. It never got better. It got worse. Much worse.

But it was NOT MY FAULT regardless. It's NOT YOUR FAULT. So stop the guilt, and know that it will only get worse. Don't fool yourself into thinking you're safer staying.

Remember this and know that there is so much more to life than to be victim to our own abuse, leaving us open and allowing abuse to become us.

Mia with her dog Blue.
A 'Book Two' story to be told.
R.I.P Blue
♥

MY DAUGHTER SAVED MY LIFE

My daughter spent countless times quietly trying to get me to see that escaping was the only way to stay alive. There were times I would listen and agree but quickly change my mind and insist we were safer staying. She was stronger than I was, seeing that leaving was the only option.

Amid a family gathering, Alen gives me a forewarning.

These signals, these warnings, were to ensure we watch our behavior or what we say and do in front of others. Here, just before he realizes I begin to take photos, I catch his true self telling me, without words, to remember what he would do if we didn't follow his rules. No one noticed these signals, these warnings. They were only meant for me, Kris and Mia at any given time. They would last only seconds, regardless of who may be around.

We always understood the warnings. It was simply part of our training. Book Two is even tougher to write, but I am writing it. I am publishing as I go to a secure site where several people have the password 'just in case'.

The story will be told.

I AM Lucy

WRITTEN BY MY DAUGHTER MIA AFTER FLEEING AN EXTREMELY ABUSIVE HOME AND FREE TO BEGIN TO SPEAK HER TRUTH AT 16 YEARS OF AGE.

I remember repeatedly telling myself that the life I was living wasn't that bad, that it could always be worse and I was overreacting to the situation. But no matter how much I convinced myself of what I considered to be fact, I still wept tears silently every night, and felt my heart and soul growing more wounds than my skin did.

If I could rip out my heart to show proof to you how damaged of a person I really am, you would see a barely beating organ, hardly recognizable as a heart by all its scars, wounds and bruises covering its face. Then, and only then, would you understand how broken my heart is. If I could show you my mind, I would. I would gather up all the broken pieces of my brain and show them to you, show you the bandages I wrapped over the pieces, trying so very hard to keep it together. I would show you the ink of every hurtful thing you ever said to me written on it, not a single piece of it still showing through the black ink, words so crowded they overlap each other time and time again.

And if I could show you my soul, you would see a fading outline of me. You would see all the bruises I ever received from you, every whip of your belt and swollen hands from the wooden spoons you would break across my palms. You would see bruised knees from when you would make us kneel for hours on end as little kids, staring at a blank wall and trying to keep it together so your anger wouldn't grow. You would see every tear that stained my cheek, every time I threw a punch against my bed or my legs as to not make noise. You would see every suicide note I failed to finish stuffed in my fist. You would see every painful word you shot at me, your words like bullets in a constantly loaded gun. You would see puffy, red eyes from endless nights of crying myself to sleep, silently as to make sure I wouldn't wake you. You'd see the tongue which I bit, holding back the truth and instead speaking lies you spun yourself, handwoven mistruths woven like a thick spider web you trapped us in.

If you could see how battered and bruised my soul is, I hope you would feel the painful sting of tears rise behind your eyes, and I hope you struggle to hold them back, so you can feel yourself choking on the pain of them. If you could see my mind, falling apart and me furiously struggling to put it back together, I hope you wouldn't be able to speak a word, for fear that if you do it would shatter to pieces like glass in front of you. And if you could see my wounded heart, I hope you hear the sound of yours cracking, breaking as you made mine do so many times.

I hope you remember seeing me as I was just a child in this world, naive and happy, running around with my brother and my mom. I hope you remember our happy smiles, and that our loud and pure laughter rings in your ears. I hope you remember when times seemed peaceful and happy, because that is exactly what it is like to live without you. I swear I have never felt a smile so bright and true on my lips, and never felt a laugh so strong and uncontrollable. Without you, I am able to wash the ink of your words off my mind, the pieces molding back together to create something whole and beautiful. Without you the cuts on my heart start to heal, the bruises slowly fade and the scars shrink down to merely tiny scratches on its surface. Without you the fist of my soul opens wide, the pieces of crumpled paper slowly slipping out of its grasp. The swelling goes down, bruises fade and scars disappear. Without you I feel like the pain you made us suffer through is falling off of me, like a heavy blanket being pulled off of a tired body, my eyes finally able to see the light so pure and bright it nearly hurts. I dare not look away, because I know that the sting in my eyes is from joy, a joy that comes with finally being able to live my life. I have a family, I found the true meaning of home. You are not a part of my family, wherever you lay is not where my home is. You chose this. This is on you. I am not just a survivor, I am a warrior.

© Mia Mango 2019

***

This is not The End.

This is just The Beginning.

***

Thank you for your support.

I AM Lucy

All Rights Reserved by the Author © Lucy Smolcic 2019

THANK YOU

September 24, 2019
On the ninth month anniversary from fleeing our abusive home, I self-published this book as an eBook.

It's been nine months since fleeing from abuse as I prepare this paperback book and we have received zero child support, zero spousal support, zero ability to sell our property or assets. My children still don't have their own beds or their belongings while Alen lives with his parents and girlfriend in the home my children and I bought and worked for. My children have been homeless and hungry, but they have been free to be themselves. The value of being able to simply be one's self is priceless.

The legal system has supported Alen in his continued abuse towards us. We have worked, actually, slaved away and own jointly the farm and all assets yet have zero ability to access them or force the sale of them to date. I will continue to battle the system, and Alen, to get what is rightfully both mine and my children's. This is not easy, but it is easier than living with the Trio and the severe abuse. It's easier than fearing for our lives on a daily basis. It's easier than never knowing when the next rage will hit while being imprisoned on a farm, isolated from everyone I once knew and loved.

It's easier but it's not right.

Thank you to all who are supporting us in so many ways. Book Two will be published sometime near Christmas 2019 or New Year 2020.

I will continue to be honest and truthful and won't be silenced any longer.

Lucy AKA Lou

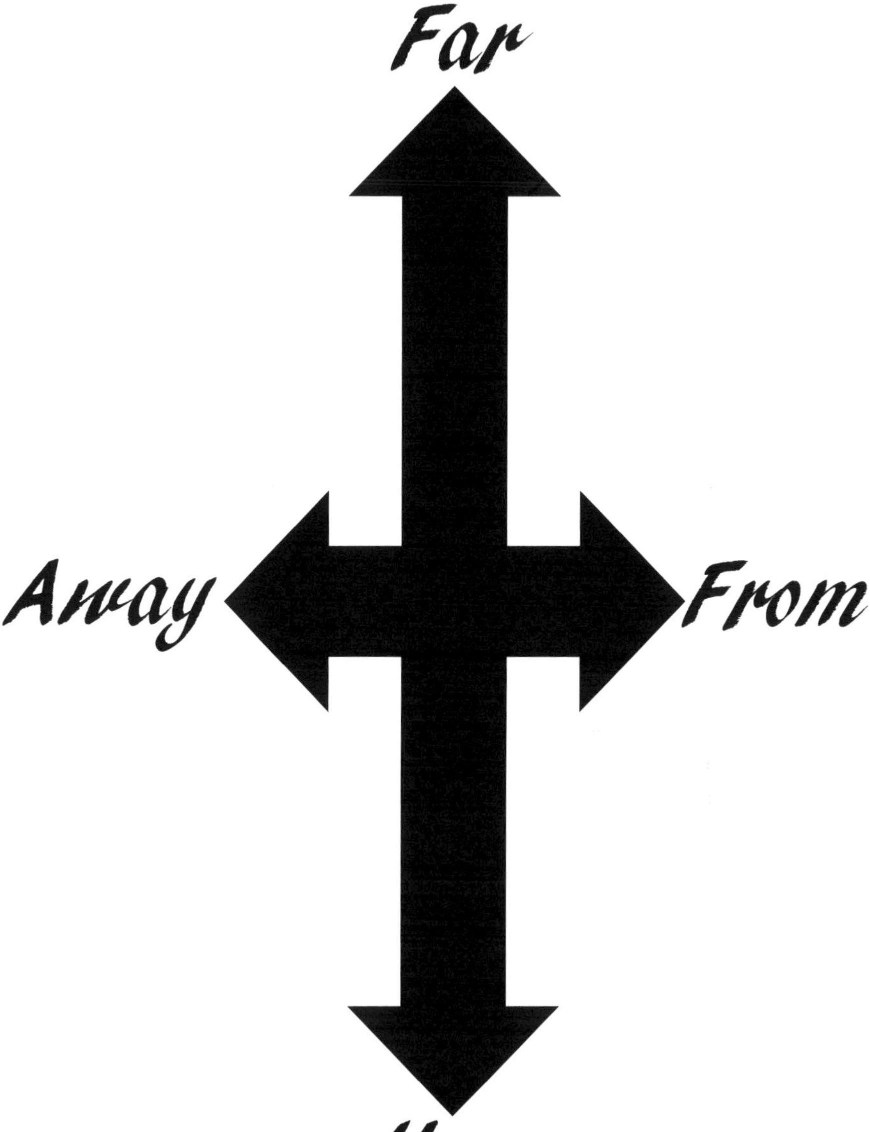
Far
Away
From
Here

I AM Lucy

Manufactured by
Amazon.ca
Bolton, ON